Abandoned

5826

261

TELCHIN, STAN

ABANDONED - WHAT IS GOD'S WILL FOR
THE JEWISH PEOPLE.....

Abandoned

What Is God's Will for
the Jewish People and the Church?

Stan Telchin

Chosen Books

A Division of Baker Book House Co
Grand Rapids, Michigan 49516

© 1997 by Stan Telchin

Published by Chosen Books
A division of Baker Book House Company
P.O. Box 6287, Grand Rapids, MI 49516-6287

Seventh printing, June 2004

Printed in the United States of America

Library of Congress Cataloging-in-Publication Data

Telchin, Stan, 1924-
    Abandoned : What is God's will for the Jewish people and the
    Church?
        p.   cm.
    Includes bibliographical references.
    ISBN 0-8007-9249-1
        1. Judaism (Christian theology) 2. Telchin, Stan, 1924-   . 3. Con-
    verts from Judaism. 4. Jewish Christians. 5. Missions to Jews. 6.
    Christianity and other religions—Judaism. 7. Judaism—Rela-
    tions—Christianity. I. Title.
    BT93.T43   1997
    261.2'6—dc20   96-33219

For current information about all releases from Baker Book House, visit our
web site:
                        http://www.bakerbooks.com

To my grandchildren,

Jennifer,
Zachary,
Elizabeth,
Nicolas.

May you live every day of your lives
knowing who you are and whose you are.

Stan Telchin Ministries
6210 N. Lockwood Ridge Rd., #143
Sarasota, FL 34243-2529
Phone: 941-907-3838
Fax: 941-907-9898
E-mail: stan@telchin.com
www.telchin.com

Contents

Foreword

I had the privilege of meeting Stan Telchin in Jerusalem on a Sunday morning in June 1995 under unusual circumstances. It was the day before the opening of the Fifth International Quadrennial Conference of the Lausanne Consultation on Jewish Evangelism. Delegates were arriving from Japan and Latin America, from Europe and the Middle East and from nearly all English-speaking nations. They came, Jews and Gentiles, because all were variously involved in the privileged task of sharing with the Jewish people the good news of Jesus Christ.

That morning a small group of us decided to go into the Old City and worship at Christ Church, identified since 1849 as a center of evangelical life and worship in the Holy Land. We went through the Jaffa Gate and started walking up to the church. But we encountered confusion—people hurrying past us in the opposite direction. Soon we, too, were turned back. Soldiers and their military vehicle dominated the scene.

We stood still, uncertain as to what to do. Some time later a shot rang out; it seemed very close. It was followed by a second shot. We could think only of terrorists. Then a third shot, startling and incongruous on what we had expected to be a quiet Sunday.

Eventually we learned that someone had left an unmarked package under one of the pews in the church. Because it might have been a bomb, the Israeli Defense Force had been alerted. Soldiers removed the package carefully, placed it in a remote corner of the plaza, off to the side of the church, drew back and opened fire. (Apparently this was the IDF approach to defusing bombs!)

The shattered package, as it turned out, proved to contain a score of Bibles, so the incident ended in laughter. And it was at that moment, as best I can recall, that I really met Stan Telchin. It was he who had laughed the loudest.

We did not go to church that day, but to the Garden Tomb not far away. Then, like typical tourists, we took pictures. I have one of Stan standing before the entrance. One might conclude, from the smile on his face, that he was thinking about the spiritual dynamite blasted to bits by Israeli gunfire. Maybe a bit of exhortation was beginning to take form in his mind: "But my Jewish brothers, you'll find that the potency of the Gospel cannot be overcome so easily. There was a time when I thought it could be reduced to mere superstition by attacking it with reason and careful research. But in the end it was Jesus who conquered me!"

Long before, I had read Stan's first book, *Betrayed!* As I read it I came to a precise conclusion: Here was a Jewish man after my own heart. Explosive in temperament, utterly candid, wonderfully open-minded, he was the sort of person one could not but be drawn to.

When his daughter Judy came to faith in Jesus, he was devastated. But over the weeks and months that followed, he had to admit she had been genuinely transformed. Rather than continue to berate her, he began to ask himself if he should face the possibility honestly that she might be right and he might be wrong.

His inherited, secondhand hostility made it impossible for him to come to any positive conclusions about Jesus of Nazareth, apart from the fact that Jesus was Jewish. Now honesty demanded that he study both Old and New Testaments and prove her wrong.

But it didn't work. Stan became convinced, in spite of himself, that Jesus was the Messiah of His people and the

Savior of the world. He surrendered himself to Jesus' Lordship and found the same release and newness that earlier had enabled Judy to courageously share with him her faith in Jesus. From then on, Stan entered on a life of widespread usefulness. Among others, he has been singularly effective in his witness to Russian Jews, leading not a few to faith.

Stan wrote this book to unburden his heart to Gentile Christians. Over the months, as he shared successive chapters with me and invited my reactions, I could not but recall the impressions that came to me years before—1939?—while listening to Hyman Appelman in Philadelphia.

I guess what first drew me and others to that Jewish evangelist was his massive street banner, *Come Hear a Jew Preach Jesus Christ!* Appelman was a gifted lawyer who could articulate the Gospel clearly and persuasively to Jews and Gentiles alike. Both he and Stan had surrendered to the same Lord Jesus and accepted the same biblical Gospel.

But the world of the '30s was different from the world of the '90s. How differently Stan proclaims the Gospel today to this generation. Between yesterday and today, the world has experienced the horrors of total war, along with the calculated destruction of six million members of European Jewry and a totally unexpected aftermath: the reemergence in Palestine, after two thousand years, of the State of Israel. Out of this tragedy and national resurrection, a contemporary voice has emerged, warm, outgoing and wonderfully in tune with the times. Stan's message is contained in this book.

Here is the contemporary note I would stress. Gentile Christians must listen to our Jewish brother in Christ. He is at rest in the wonders of his faith in Jesus, the Messiah of His people. Further, Stan rejoices in his God-given Jewishness, which I believe is most pleasing to God and reflects

11

a reality that is altogether refreshing. One is put at ease in his presence and cannot but resonate with his efforts to receive all those whom God has manifestly received.

In this book, a deeply committed Jewish believer reaches over the mountains of Gentile barbarism and "Christian" anti-Semitism that destroyed many of his people, and speaks in a friendly fashion to Gentile Christians about his people. I believe I know the measure of his heart and the depth of his concern. When he asked me to comment freely on the rough drafts of his successive chapters, what could I say? Little but my oft-repeated words, "Stan, this is great! Your strength is the note of reality that breaks through in your thoughts, your words, your style. Thank God you are not pompous! You don't talk down to Gentile Christians. You come across as a brother and friend with something truly important to share."

So then, this book. It is not enough that those of us who are Gentile Christians should "bow down in worship, . . . [and] kneel before the Lord our Maker" (Psalm 95:6). We should at the same time reach out in love to the people who are always on God's heart. He loves the Jewish people, despite the tragic persistence with which so many continue to say no to His Son. We should love them, too, displaying our love in every way, especially the way Stan loves them.

And this means we should likewise embrace the implications of the apostle Paul's inspired word that the Gospel "is the power of God unto salvation . . . to the Jew first" (Romans 1:16, KJV).

Arthur F. Glasser
Fuller Theological Seminary
Dean Emeritus, School of World Mission
Professor Emeritus, Theology and East Asian Studies
Faculty Coordinator of Judaic Studies

Special Thanks

First and foremost, I thank God for His grace and the inspiration He provided as this book was being born.

A number of special people helped make this book a joy to write. My ever-present wife, Ethel, is first in line. She was wonderfully encouraging and patiently endured those long times alone when I was working. She also read and commented on every chapter, cheerfully and insightfully.

Moishe Rosen also deserves special recognition. Moishe is the guy who insisted that while there was still life in me, I had to write this book. He has been to me a wonderful example of a man who has laid it all on the line for the Lord.

Thanks, too, to Dr. Arthur F. Glasser, whose advice and guidance during the long writing period were invaluable.

Bob Mendelsohn, James Rankin, Clark Tyler and John Bayles also deserve special mention for their loving encouragement.

I especially want to thank Jane Campbell at Chosen Books, my editor, who labored with me to continually sharpen my focus.

My sincere thanks to each of these and to the many other friends who prayed that "the anointing of God would be all over me" as I wrote this book.

An Introductory Word

Telchin, you must write another book!" People have been saying this to me for a number of years now. My friends say it. My publisher says it. People who have read my first book, *Betrayed!,* say it. You may have said it. And, yes, I have heard the urging. But I was waiting for a different kind of prompting. And now it has come.

I am a first-generation American Jew who is very happy with his Jewishness and his heritage. I am also a devoted follower of Messiah Jesus. I have no trouble living joyfully with both of these identities.

Having said that, I must also say this: If you don't believe in God, you won't enjoy reading this book. If you don't believe the Bible is God's Word, then the issues this book raises will seem at best only interesting to you. If you don't believe Jesus is the Messiah whose coming was prophesied throughout the Hebrew Scriptures, then you won't fully understand much of what you will be reading. If you don't believe Satan is active in this world, then a critically important thesis within this book may seem laughable to you. I tell you these things not to dissuade you from reading this book, but to help you understand where I am coming from as I write it.

Having said that, I invite you to read on.

More than 21 years have passed since I was first confronted with the question "Is Jesus the Jewish Messiah?" In my first book I explained that I did everything I could think of to disprove His Messiahship. But in the end, from my study of Scripture, I was finally convinced: Jesus is

15

our Messiah. The ensuing years have added to and developed my conviction in many wonderful ways.

For fourteen years I served as pastor of a New Covenant congregation made up of Jews and Gentiles—people of every color, size and shape. I saw what happens when individuals from different walks of life, backgrounds and races consciously put an end to self-centeredness by receiving Jesus as Lord of their lives. Determined to live in obedience to biblical teaching, they also put off their often deeply ingrained prejudices and work wholeheartedly with others who have made the same decision.

Over those years I learned many things about how believers in Yeshua (the Hebrew name of Jesus) are to live their lives together. I also learned much about God's will for His chosen people. So I feel especially qualified to address a subject many people do not understand and many others are reluctant to address: the present urgent need for believers in Yeshua to reach out to and receive the Jewish people.

It is my hope that the information you are about to receive will help you understand how important you are in God's plan to reach the Jewish people with His message of love, and that it will equip you to do so more effectively.

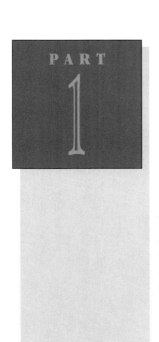

PART

1

Information
You Need

In this section I will present some things you need to know—about our universe, about the Bible, about Church history . . . and about me.

1

"We Can't Afford to Lose You!"

That's what she said when she called: "We can't afford to lose you!"

As clearly as I can remember, her call came in about 10:30 the first Friday morning in August 1975. That's a long time ago. You might ask, "What was so important in what she said? Why do you remember it to this day?" It was important because when I understood what she was really saying, I was challenged to the core of my being.

Let me explain. In my first book, *Betrayed!,* I pointed out that I accepted Jesus as my Messiah at about 7:15 A.M. on July 3, 1975. By August the word had spread. I didn't take out any ads in *The Washington Post* or go on radio or TV with the announcement. But somehow the word had gotten around that "Stan Telchin has been born again. Now he calls himself a messianic Jew, but he's really a Christian."

Surely you've heard it said, "It's not what you know that counts; it's who you know." Well, sometimes it isn't even who you know that counts, but who knows you.

The woman who called—let's call her Shirley—wasn't a close friend of mine. Rather, we were colleagues. She was a Chartered Life Underwriter. So was I. She was a member of the Million Dollar Round Table. So was I. We always greeted each other warmly whenever we met and our relationship was cordial. But we were more than colleagues. Shirley was also Jewish, and for a number of years we had worked together on various boards of Jewish organizations in and around Washington, D.C. It was the Jewishness we shared, rather than the professional basis of our friendship, that prompted her to make the call that Friday morning.

And I've got to tell you, I was taken aback.

"What are you talking about, Shirley?" I asked. "What do you mean, 'We can't afford to lose you'? What are you saying?"

"You know what I mean! Let me ask you directly: Is what I hear true?"

"I don't know what you're talking about. What have you heard?"

"Come on, Stan, don't try to be cute with me. Is it true you've become a Christian?"

How was I supposed to answer this question? Was I supposed to start arguing semantics? Was I supposed to say, "No, it isn't true; I haven't become a Christian, but a messianic Jew"?

These responses did race through my head as I heard the iciness of her voice. I'm not sure what I actually did say, but it was probably along the lines of, "Now, wait a minute, Shirley. If you're asking if it's true that I now believe that Jesus is our Messiah, then the answer is yes. But you haven't lost me. I'm not going anywhere. I'm the same guy I've always been. I'm still Jewish!"

I stopped to catch my breath. There was a long pause. Then Shirley said again, "Oh, Stan, this is terrible. We really can't afford to lose you. Won't you reconsider what you've done?"

Another long pause. Then I said, "Shirley, I've done a lot of studying and a lot of soul-searching, and I truly believe that Jesus is our Messiah. If that doesn't sit well with you, I'm sorry."

At that, and without a good-bye, Shirley hung up.

I cannot express how I felt at that moment. It was very long ago. But the fact that I still remember the conversation should help you understand the impact it had on me.

Us and Them

I shouldn't have been surprised. After all, I was not a kid. I was one month shy of celebrating my 51st birthday. And I was a first-generation American whose parents came from Russia in the early 1900s to escape the pogroms. If you've seen *Fiddler on the Roof,* you know what I mean.

When I first saw that play, I felt it had been written about my family. My parents were like the couple in *Fiddler.* They fled Russia to get away from the organized persecution and massacre of Jewish people rampant there. My father, grandfather and uncles came to New York City in 1904 with little more than the clothes on their backs. Even though they did not know English, they were soon able to get work to support themselves. Two years later they had saved enough to bring my mother, grandmother and assorted aunts and cousins to the United States. Included in the group was my brother Charlie, who had been born in Russia after my father left.

21

Over the next eighteen years, five more children were born into our family. On September 14, 1924, I was born, the youngest and smallest member of the family.

Until I reached age six, we lived on the Lower East Side of New York, where I began to learn about Jewish ghetto life in America and about discrimination and prejudice.

In kindergarten I was called a Christ-killer for the first time. I didn't know what that expression meant, but I knew I didn't do it. The hatred in the accusation frightened me more than the words. I remember rushing up the stairs to our sixth-floor tenement apartment at 35 Market Street in Manhattan, just a few blocks from the Williamsburg Bridge, crying, "Mama, Mama!"

I don't remember the exact words my mother used to comfort me, but she probably spoke partially in Yiddish and partially in broken English.

"*Zunnela*, my little son, don't cry. Let me tell you something very important that you have to learn. There is 'us,' the Jewish people, and there is 'them,' the *goyim,* the Christians. They hate us and we have to stay away from them. Everything is all right now. Stop crying. No one is going to hurt you. We are in America and you are safe. Just stay away from them."

As clearly as I can remember, the next thing she did was give me a glass of cold chocolate milk.

When I was nine we moved to Brooklyn, into what was still pretty much of a ghetto. Forty percent of the people in Boro Park were Jewish and forty percent were Catholic, with the remaining twenty percent made up of all others. Our block, 43rd Street between Fort Hamilton Parkway and Twelfth Avenue, was about 85 percent Jewish.

We lived at 1143–43rd Street. While not a six-story tenement, it was a four-story walk-up. No elevator. We had a four-room apartment—kitchen, living room, two bedrooms and a bathroom. While there were six kids in our family, only three of us at the time lived at home. Mom and Pop shared a bedroom, my brother Sam and I shared a bedroom, and my sister Dorris slept on a folding bed in the living room–dining room.

We were crowded, as you can imagine. Bathroom time was sometimes crisis time. But it was 1933, the middle of the Depression, and things were tough out there in the real world. Fortunately Pop and three of my brothers were able to find work, so we managed. But that doesn't mean we escaped the anti-Semitism present everywhere.

One hot summer Sunday morning I was playing stickball in the schoolyard at Public School 131 at Fort Hamilton Parkway and 43rd Street. It was almost noon and our game was over. As I walked home from the schoolyard, dressed only in shorts and sneakers, I saw this lady heading right for me—a large woman dressed completely in black, wearing a black hat and carrying a black purse.

The closer she got to me, the more I noticed her piercing look. It frightened me. I remember stopping in my tracks. I didn't know what to do. She kept coming right at me.

As she got up to me, she hit me in the chest with her big, black pocketbook and said, "Get out of my way, you dirty little kike!"

I fell to the sidewalk in total amazement. Then I started to cry. I got up and ran the hundred yards to our apartment house. As I ran up the steps, I was crying, "Mama, Mama!"

Once again my mother had to comfort me. And again she reminded me that there is "us" and there is "them," the *goyim,* the Christians. They hate us. And the best thing we can do is stay away from them.

So Shirley's comment that Friday morning in August 1975 had a significant impact on me. What she was really saying was, "You are no longer part of *us.* You have become part of *them.*"

What about the Messiah?

I described in considerable detail in *Betrayed!* the struggle I went through when I was first compelled to consider the question "Is Jesus the Jewish Messiah?" If you haven't read that book, you might want to obtain a copy. But I will retell parts of the story now, because it sets the stage for all that follows.

The first time I ever heard the word *Messiah* used, I think I was about seven, in the midst of the Depression. I asked my mother for a new bike, something we definitely could not afford. She told me laughingly that I could have it "ven der Meshiach kumt" (when the Messiah comes). I wasn't sure what that meant, but I knew I would not be getting the bike I had asked for.

The next time I heard the word *Messiah* was when news of the Holocaust exploded in our midst. I was about sixteen. I heard my mother praying and asking God to send the Messiah to deliver us from the hatred of the world.

Though my grandparents were ultra-Orthodox, my parents were more conservative in their observance of Jewish customs and rituals. We often went to the synagogue, but I can't remember my parents ever really talking with me about God. And we never talked about the Messiah. We talked about what we could and could not do.

We also assumed that anyone who wasn't Jewish was automatically Christian. I learned from the experiences I have described, and many others, that the farther I stayed away from "them," the easier my life would be.

Meet the Love of My Life

Now let me tell you about Ethel. I first met her when she became a student at Montauk Junior High School, located on 16th Avenue between 42nd and 43rd Streets in Brooklyn. I was in the eighth grade. She was a brand-new seventh-grader. We worked on the newspaper together. We were also in the band. (I played trumpet; she played flute.) But although we came to know each other, we weren't really close friends. Later we went to different high schools and didn't see much of each other.

Then came the Army. In December 1944, just before I went overseas in World War II, I was home on furlough and went to visit Helen, a good friend of mine whose husband was in the service, too. I had been there only about an hour when the doorbell rang. It was Ethel. She, too, had come to visit Helen.

Later, as we were leaving Helen's apartment, I asked her if I could walk her home. We walked and walked and talked and talked. Then, as we were parting, Ethel asked me if I wanted her to write to me.

"What a question!" I replied.

"Good! And I'll send you some packages."

Fifteen months later, when the war was over and I was discharged, I went to Ethel's house to thank her for her letters and packages. She looked wonderful to me! We had our first date the very next day, and two years later, on May 26, 1948, we married.

Ethel is a very special lady and we have had an exceptionally happy marriage. We have also been blessed with two beautiful daughters, Judy and Ann. Then there were the material things. Twenty-six years into our marriage, we had a large home complete with swimming pool, four BMWs and a full-time housekeeper. I was very successful financially.

Then my world came apart. Judy, who was then a student at Boston University, called me one Sunday evening. From the moment I picked up the phone, I sensed something wrong. In our 45-minute conversation, Judy said she had come to believe that Jesus is the Messiah. I was almost speechless. Outraged. I felt betrayed. How could a child of mine join the enemy?

As the conversation continued, I realized I had two options: I could disown her immediately for this terrible act, or I could love her through it. I decided on the second.

Two weeks later Judy came home for her spring vacation. We talked a lot. I don't remember much of what Judy said, but I remember that I kept saying, "But Judy, you're Jewish! You can't be Jewish and believe in Jesus."

To which she replied, "Daddy, that isn't true. Some Jews have always believed in Jesus."

Just before returning to school, Judy challenged me to do something I had never done.

"You're an educated man," she said. "You have all sorts of degrees. Read the Bible for yourself and make up your own mind. It's either true or it's false. And if you read it carefully, Daddy, and ask God to reveal the truth to you, He will."

I understood what Judy wanted to accomplish by that challenge, but I saw it as a way to disprove what she believed. So I decided immediately to read the Bible and gather enough information to prove that Jesus is *not* the Messiah. By doing so, I would win her back.

My Study Begins

After dinner the next night I picked up the New Testament for the very first time. As I set out to read the book of Matthew, I was prepared for a book of hate aimed at the Jewish people. What else could it be? *The Christians get their hate for us either from their mother's milk or from this book,* I thought.

But I didn't find it to be a book of hate. It was a book written by a Jew, for other Jews, about the God of Abraham, Isaac and Jacob and the Messiah He had sent to His people. The next night, a Tuesday, I read the book of Mark. On Wednesday night I read Luke. On Thursday and Friday nights I read John. My notepad was filling up with lots and lots of questions. On Saturday morning I began to read the Acts of the Apostles.

All went well until I came to the tenth chapter of this book. There I read about Peter going reluctantly to the house of Cornelius, the Roman centurion—a Gentile. Peter didn't want to be there with this Gentile. But Cornelius explained that he had had a vision in which he learned that Peter would tell him about God.

With that prompting, and since Peter had had a corroborating vision, he began to tell Cornelius about the God of Abraham, Isaac and Jacob and about Jesus, the Messiah. And while Peter was speaking, something totally unexpected happened: The Holy Spirit fell on Cornelius and on all the Gentiles in his home.

Peter and the Jewish believers with him were astonished. How could this be? How could the Holy Spirit fall on these Gentiles? The Holy Spirit of God had been given to the Jews, not the Gentiles.

Then, in the very next chapter of Acts, I read about Peter attending a meeting of Jewish believers in Jerusalem. They were upset with him because he had broken bread with a Gentile and shared the Messiah with him and his family. Peter explained what had happened and how the Holy Spirit had fallen on the Gentiles in Cornelius' house. At this report, the believers decided that God is no respecter of persons and that Jesus the Messiah must be for Gentiles as well as Jews.

As I read these things, I was stunned. How was it possible that two thousand years ago Jesus was only for us Jews and not for Gentiles, and now He is only for Gentiles and not for us? What had happened over the years?

As I set out to study the matter, I wrote down a series of significant questions, each of which led to the next:

Do I really believe in God?

Do I believe the Tenach (the entire Hebrew Bible) is God's Word to us, or is it only a human account of the Jewish people?

Does the Tenach contain prophecies about a Messiah who is to come?

Has anyone ever lived who fulfilled these prophecies?

Did Jesus fulfill them?

If I received a "no" answer to any of these questions, I knew my study would be over. But if each question produced a "yes," I would be in serious trouble, because the last thing in the world I wanted to believe was that Jesus is our Jewish Messiah!

The next days, weeks and months were filled with study. After a few days I took a leave of absence from my business so I could have more time to study. I read the entire New Covenant and a good portion of the Tenach. I went to the library and obtained books about Jewish religion and history. I talked to rabbis. And I studied the messianic prophecies in the Tenach.

I had no idea how many prophecies the Tenach contained, but I came up with a list of more than forty of them. It staggered me to recognize (as I was beginning to do) that Jesus fulfilled each and every one of them.

Particularly significant to me in my study of Scripture was Jeremiah 31:31–34, in which God promised to make a new covenant with the Jewish people. How could I have been fifty years old and not known of this promise?

Then there was Proverbs 30, which spoke of God's Son; and Psalm 22, which revealed the Messiah hanging on a tree; and Isaiah 53, which explained that our sins were placed on Him and that He was punished in our stead; and Daniel 9, which prophesied that Jerusalem would be destroyed along with the Temple by the prince who would come, and that this destruction would take place after the Messiah had been cut off. By now I knew when these things had taken place. They happened in the year 70 C.E.

This realization stunned me. "Either the Messiah came and died before the year 70," I wrote, "or else the Bible is merely the story of the Jewish people and not the Word of God." The more I thought about the Scriptures I had been studying, the more convinced I became that Jesus really is the Jewish Messiah.

But that was something I did not want to acknowledge, much less believe.

Whom Do You Worship?

Months into my study, I decided to attend a meeting of "messianic" Jews—Jews who believe Jesus is the Messiah. At this meeting I met a woman named Lillian who, when she found out that I was not yet a believer in Jesus, offered me her Bible and asked me to read Exodus 20:2–3 aloud.

I opened her Bible and read, "I am the LORD your God, who brought you out of the land of Egypt, out of the house of bondage. You shall have no other gods before me" (RSV).

When I finished reading, Lillian asked me to close the Bible. Then she said, "Tell me, Stan, who is your God? Is He the God of our fathers—the God of Abraham, Isaac and Jacob? Or are you worshiping false gods like your business, your home, your wife, your children? What do you spend your time thinking about? Whom do you worship?"

I was struck by Lillian's questions and realized that I spent a good part of my time thinking and even worshiping these things. I almost never thought about God or considered worshiping Him.

Lillian's questions did their work. The pressure within me kept building. Now I knew that in my heart I believed Jesus is the Messiah, but I was afraid to confess it with my mouth. I feared the consequences such a decision would have on my life, on the life of my family and on my business. I remember arguing with myself, raising the objections of the Crusades and the Inquisition and the pogroms and the Holocaust.

But as if to answer each argument, on the inside of me I would hear, *Yes, but it's true. Jesus is the Messiah.*

The day after I talked with Lillian, on July 3, 1975, at 7:15 in the morning, it finally burst forth from my lips: "Jesus is our Messiah! He is my Messiah! I do receive Him as the Lord of my life."

And Now?

I have studied the Scriptures diligently in the years since then. You must know that if I was convinced in 1975 that Jesus is who He declared Himself to be, I am even more convinced today.

But I am convinced about some other things, too—specifically, God's will for the Jewish people and for the Church.

So here is what I intend to do in the pages that follow. I will shed light on what may still be darkness in your life. I will help you understand part of the purposes of God for our generation. I will point out some of the mistakes the Church has made over the years, so that none of us will remain blind. And I want us all to hear and respond to the urging of God to reach out to and receive His covenant people.

CHAPTER 2

The Greatest Battle in the Universe

In just a minute I will talk with you about what I believe is the greatest battle in the universe. But before I do, I've got to share something personal with you—how uncomfortable I felt on those infrequent occasions when, before I became a believer, I had to enter a church building.

This preconditioning did not disappear immediately when I accepted the Lord. I remember what happened, for example, when I visited St. Timothy's Episcopal Church in Catonsville, Maryland, then pastored by the Reverend Philip Zampino.

As a believer I admired many of the wonderful things I had learned about Phil Zampino. He was a gentle man in whom I saw tremendous spirituality. He also loved the Jewish people and prayed for us frequently. Soon after we met for the first time, I learned that he was conducting his fifth tour to Israel. I was impressed. Even though he wore "their" collar and clothes, this man did not seem like one of "them."

Over the months I went to a number of meetings at which Father Zampino spoke, and we came to know one another. When he learned of my background, he asked if I would come to Catonsville on a Sunday evening to speak at his church.

And here's the point: I will never forget how uncomfortable I felt when I entered St. Timothy's for the first time. It was so large and . . . *Gothic!* And there were those large, "Christian," stained-glass windows all around the room! Then I looked at the pulpit from which I would be speaking. It had a big cross on it.

The first words that came out of my mouth after I had been introduced were, "Please forgive me, but I am so uncomfortable, I want to run out of this place."

I did not, of course. I went on to speak, and later met some of the good people of that congregation.

But I am not the only Jew to have felt that way, not by a long stretch. Because most Jewish people have little or no knowledge of the New Covenant, they do not perceive the cross in its biblical sense—the place where the Messiah took our sins on Himself, was punished in our stead and shed His blood so we could enter into our New Covenant relationship with God. Rather, most Jewish people see the cross as the symbol of all of the persecution we have experienced at the hands of Christians over the centuries.

The same lack of knowledge keeps most Jewish people from understanding what the Church and Christians were meant to be.

In the decades since July 3, 1975, when I first confessed Jesus as Lord of my life, I have learned many truths from Scripture. Truths about God. Truths about Jesus and about why He came to earth, lived, died and rose again. Truths about the Jewish people. Truths about Satan. But underlying all these truths is one fundamental fact: The greatest battle in the universe is the one between God and Satan over the wills of men and women, boys and girls. Later in this book I will deal with this subject in considerable detail. But in this chapter I simply want to introduce it and provide a brief overview.

God's Covenant with the Jewish People

Throughout the Bible we learn that God has made some very specific promises to the Jewish people. We see one such promise in Jeremiah 31:

> This is what the LORD says, he who appoints the sun to shine by day, who decrees the moon and stars to shine by night, who stirs up the sea so that its waves roar—the LORD Almighty is his name: "Only if these decrees vanish from my sight," declares the LORD, "will the descendants of Israel ever cease to be a nation before me."
>
> verses 35–36

Dwell on this wonderful promise. Read it aloud to yourself. Think about it.

In the preface I said that if you don't believe Satan is active in this world, then a critically important thesis within this book may seem laughable. I repeat that statement here and offer that thesis: Satan hates God and wants to do everything he can to discredit Him. Because God has promised that the Jewish people will be a nation before Him so long as the sun shines by day and the moon and stars by night, Satan wants to nullify this promise by destroying the Jewish people and removing them from the earth. He must think that if he succeeds in destroying the Jewish people, he will prove God a liar.

Now I call your attention to the Covenant God promised a few verses earlier in Jeremiah 31:

> "The time is coming," declares the LORD, "when I will make a new covenant with the house of Israel and with the house of Judah. It will not be like the covenant I made with their forefathers when I took them by the hand to lead them out of Egypt, because they broke my covenant, though I was a husband to them," declares the LORD.
>
> verses 31–32

Here are some specifics of this New Covenant:

> "This is the covenant I will make with the house of Israel after that time," declares the LORD. "I will put my law in their minds and write it on their hearts. I will be their God, and they will be my people. No longer will a man teach his neighbor, or a man his brother, saying, 'Know the LORD,' because they will all know me, from the least of them to the greatest," declares the LORD. "For I will forgive their wickedness and will remember their sins no more."
>
> verses 33–34

Just before Jesus died for the sins of the world, He inaugurated this New Covenant at the last Passover meal with His totally Jewish disciples. At the end of the meal, He raised the cup and said, "This cup is the new covenant in my blood, which is poured out for you" (Luke 22:20).

How Satan Tries to Change God's Promise

God commands the Church to share the New Covenant message of salvation with the Jewish people so that they, too, can be saved. He wants the Church, by her unity and joy in Him as well as by her obedience to His will, to "provoke [the Jewish people] to jealousy" (Romans 11:11, KJV) so that they will want to receive the Messiah. This is a critical truth that I will explore in considerable detail in chapter 12.

But we must also be crystal-clear in our understanding that Satan, in order to counteract God's will, wants the Church to provoke the Jewish people of the world not to jealousy but to fear and anger, so that they will not want to receive the Messiah. Satan wants Jewish people to experience the wrath of God, so he tries to convince them—and people in the Church—that the New Covenant is for Gentiles only.

Nine Unscriptural Attitudes

To accomplish his will, Satan has successfully planted unscriptural attitudes in the hearts and minds of many Christians. Let me share nine of these with you:

1. The only good Jew is a dead or converted Jew. (This cruel slogan was popular during the Inquisition of the late fifteenth century.)
2. When a Jew receives Jesus as Lord and Savior, he or she stops being Jewish.
3. God is through with the Jewish people because they had their chance and blew it.
4. The Jewish people have suffered over these past two thousand years because they crucified Jesus.
5. Jews who believe in Jesus should be segregated from Gentile Christians and not be part of the Church.
6. The Great Commission to carry the Gospel to the uttermost parts of the earth does not include sharing with Jewish neighbors and friends in the next

office or down the block. Why not? Because the Jewish people no longer matter to God.

7. The Jewish people suffered enough in the Holocaust, and the Church should just leave them alone.
8. The Jewish people have their own Sinaitic covenant with God and need to live in accordance with the Law of Moses, just as the Church needs to live under the New Covenant.
9. A person born Jewish should remain Jewish and not seek to become a Christian.

The voice of Satan can be heard in each of these statements. The attitudes they generate and the actions to which they lead have his imprint all over them. These attitudes and actions have hurt Jewish people and Gentile Christians alike over the centuries.

Lack of Sensitivity

Satan has not misled only those believers who leave Jewish people alone. He plants unscriptural attitudes in other Christians, too. Some do not accept new Jewish believers as brothers or sisters in the Lord, but see them as "former Jews." Other Christians, meeting a Jewish believer for the first time, act as if he or she is their new mascot. They want to coddle him and show him off.

All too often—most of the time, in fact—Gentile Christians demonstrate a lack of sensitivity concerning the deeply ingrained fears of the new Jewish believer: fear of the cross, fear of the Church, fear of Christians in general. I will have much to say about this in chapter 13.

Another example of insensitivity involves Jewish holidays. Many messianic Jews are frustrated when Gentile believers disregard the holidays that are such a part of most of our lives. Rosh Hashanah, Yom Kippur, Passover,

Pentecost and the rest of our holidays had tremendous importance to Jesus, to each of the disciples and to all Jewish believers in the days when the Church was basically a Jewish sect.

But over the years, as more and more Gentiles came into the Church, these holidays began to lose their meaning, so that today many Gentile congregations see no need to celebrate such distinctive "Jewish" events. How far the Church has gone to forget and even repudiate her Jewish roots!

Still more insensitivity is demonstrated when negative references to Jews are made by Christians. These references ring alarm bells for us—and I don't mean only flat-out anti-Semitic remarks. Let me share a personal story to illustrate what I mean.

Some years ago a fairly well-known Bible teacher was conducting a study on the book of Galatians. A friend of mine gave me a set of his tapes and I set out eagerly to listen to them. Over the next few days I listened to all of them in my car. But every time I heard this minister use the term *Judaizers*, I reacted on the inside. I knew who the Judaizers were—those Jewish people in the first century who said Gentiles had to be circumcised and come under the Law in order to become followers of Messiah Jesus.

But the venom I heard in this Bible teacher's voice as he said the word *Judaizers* reflected a tone I had heard my whole life when someone blurted out the word *Jew!* And his animosity toward the Judaizers, I feared, would be perceived by his students as the appropriate animosity they should have for us "Jews."

I know this excellent Bible teacher did not intend to convey such a perception. But he could have avoided it entirely if, in the course of his explanation of the term *Judaizers*, he had thought to take just thirty seconds to explain that he was *not* talking about the Jewish people as a whole, then or now.

My Purpose in Sharing These Things

Do these unscriptural attitudes and insensitivities (perhaps unintentional or the result of wrong teaching) mean that Jewish believers should segregate themselves in synagogues, avoid Gentile churches and have nothing to do with Gentile believers? Not at all. This would cater to and reinforce these fears. Rather, I have highlighted the insensitive attitudes and actions within some churches to stress that they have come from neither God nor His Word. And only when they are exposed and dealt with will the offenses they cause be brought to an end.

What is God's will in this matter? The apostle Paul, in his letter to the Ephesians, reminded the early Gentile believers to understand their spiritual roots. He also stressed that they were not to separate themselves from one another. Here is the instruction he gave to both Jewish and Gentile believers:

> Make every effort to keep the unity of the Spirit through the bond of peace. There is one body and one Spirit—just as you were called to one hope when you were called— one Lord, one faith, one baptism; one God and Father of all, who is over all and through all and in all.
>
> Ephesians 4:3–6

I started this chapter by stressing an underlying truth: that the greatest battle in the universe is the battle between God and Satan over the wills of men and women. I also noted that Satan is trying to destroy the Jewish people in order to make God out to be a liar. If he cannot destroy them physically, he tries to keep them away from Messiah Jesus so that they will not be able to experience the grace of God that comes from receiving Jesus as Lord. He would love for them to experience the curse of the Law and the wrath that is to come.

But God is moving mightily today among Jewish people all over the world. This is one reason I believe (with many others) that we are in the end times. And Christians in every nation and denomination need to recognize what God is doing so they can work together to accomplish His will. This requires us as individuals to decide that working together is the will of God. It requires us to increase our own understanding of Jewish people and what they believe about God, the Bible, Jesus and Christians. It requires us to prepare our own hearts to reach out to and receive Jewish people. And it requires us to understand what God has declared awaits the people of the world, including Jewish people, if they reject His Son, the Messiah.

This increased understanding must go beyond our minds and into our hearts, so that we will be motivated by love for the Jewish people as well as by a desire to obey the Lord.

We are accountable for no one else's decision concerning Messiah Jesus. Whether anyone accepts or rejects Him is up to him or her. But we *are* accountable for our obedience to the Great Commission. We must never forget that the Gospel "is the power of God for the salvation of everyone who believes: first for the Jew, then for the Gentile" (Romans 1:16).

One additional truth. As we approach the end the twentieth century, it is easier to speak with Jewish people about Jesus than at any time in the last 1,900 years. But this does not mean reaching Jewish people is easy. We must not expect, just because the hearts of Gentile believers have changed toward the Jewish people, that Jewish hearts have changed toward Christians or Christianity. What the Church has done over the past two thousand years cannot be reversed in a month or a year or even a decade. Over the centuries the issue has rarely been Jesus—who He is and what He did for the Jewish people in His life, death and resurrection. The issue has been the persecution of Jews by "Christians" who brandished the cross and tried to force us into their churches.

But that is not an excuse to stall. So let's begin by addressing the problem as it exists today.

CHAPTER 3

Reading the Rest of Romans

A number of years ago, during a class in Church history, the professor asked if we students had developed a philosophy of history based on Romans 9, 10 and 11. Most of us did not know what he was talking about. As for the answer to his question, that was beyond us, particularly when he added, "If you don't understand how these three chapters affect our lives today, you won't understand a critically important aspect of biblical truth."

I have often thought of this professor's words and the stress he placed on chapters 9–11 of Paul's great letter to the Romans. Why? Because we often forget one of the most remarkable attributes of God: His faithfulness.

God is often described as the covenant-making and covenant-keeping God. But do we in the Church today perceive His faithfulness to His covenant with the physical descendants of Abraham, Isaac and Jacob? Do we see His faithfulness to the Jewish people only in the older Covenant—that is, in Old Testament times? Do we assume God stopped being faithful to them in the era of the New Covenant and the Church? Does He no longer have a plan and purpose for those He once called "the apple of His eye" (Deuteronomy 32:10)? Has He discarded the Jews?

In this chapter I intend to contrast biblical teaching on God's relationship with the Jewish people with the assumptions of many in the Church. To do this, let's look at the *rest* of the book of Romans.

"Do Not Be Ignorant of This Mystery"

Anyone who reads Romans 1–8 becomes increasingly aware of the wonder of God's salvation through Messiah Jesus. Paul begins with God's indictment of the appalling sin of the human race (1:18–3:20). Then he explains God's abounding grace to sinners through the Messiah (3:21–5:21), in whom He has provided eternal salvation. Paul goes on to speak of God's abounding grace toward those who have turned to Jesus in repentance and faith (6:1–8:39). Through the cross and the Holy Spirit, God has made salvation not just a future hope but a present reality.

Some of Paul's key verses are terrific! What Christian has not been thrilled with the joyous opening verses of chapter 8?

> Therefore, there is now no condemnation for those who are in Christ Jesus, because through Christ Jesus the law of the Spirit of life set me free from the law of sin and death.
>
> verses 1–2

"Amen! Hallelujah! We are no longer condemned. We are set free. Praise the Lord!"

What about verses 16 and 17?

> The Spirit himself testifies with our spirit that we are God's children. Now if we are children, then we are heirs—heirs of God and co-heirs with Christ.
>
> verses 16–17

"Oh, yes! Amen! Praise the Lord! The Bible says it, I believe it and that settles it!"

And what about this terrific promise?

> We know that in all things God works for the good of those who love him, who have been called according to his purpose.
>
> verse 28

"Yes! Give me a high five! No matter how tough things get, God is at work in the midst of them. And all things are going to work together for my good because I love God and am called according to His purpose."

> What, then, shall we say in response to this? If God is for us, who can be against us?
>
> verse 31

"Hallelujah!"

> He who did not spare his own Son, but gave him up for us all—how will he not also, along with him, graciously give us all things?
>
> verse 32

"It's true! The Bible says it and I believe it."

In all these things we are more than conquerors through him who loved us.

verse 37

"Yes! That's the grace of God to us."

For I am convinced that neither death nor life, neither angels nor demons, neither the present nor the future, nor any powers, neither height nor depth, nor anything else in all creation, will be able to separate us from the love of God that is in Christ Jesus our Lord.

verses 38–39

"Oh, yes! It's true! And it's wonderful!"

But what comes next? More wonderful, exciting truth? Not a bit. Suddenly we encounter a different Paul, one who has "great sorrow and unceasing anguish in [his] heart" (Romans 9:2). Paul is overwhelmed by the unthinkable. Something has happened to Israel that fills him with dismay:

I do not want you to be ignorant of this mystery, brothers, so that you may not be conceited: Israel has experienced a hardening in part until the full number of the Gentiles has come in.

Romans 11:25

These 36 words are among the most profound in the book of Romans. Read them again slowly. They present a message for the Church today. Indeed, they challenge believers worldwide.

Now read them aloud and listen as you read. As you do, you will hear the voice of God speaking directly to you.

Please, brothers and sisters, don't be "ignorant of this mystery," thinking that knowing *about* the Gospel is all that matters. Don't be "conceited," thinking you are smarter than unbelieving Jewish people because you believe the Gospel. Otherwise you will wind up in your own foolishness, forgetting you are to glorify God with your mind as well as your heart. Don't be narrow-minded, thinking only of your own family and friends and remaining indifferent to the unevangelized.

Although the eyes of some Jewish people have been opened to see Jesus, the Light of the world, the eyes of most Jewish people remain blind. But this, according to Paul, is for a limited time, awaiting "the full number of the Gentiles" who are to be saved.

Think about these things carefully. And when you think you've got it—really got it—you will be ready to hear more of what God is saying to His people today. It is a message most of the Church seems not to have heard. Many believers, despite Paul's warning, have become "wise in [their] own conceits" (Romans 12:16, KJV). But God wants the piercing light of His truth to burn away those conceits, so we can hear the message He has for us today.

The Truth God Wants Us to Learn

Just what is the message God wants us to hear?

All Israel will be saved, as it is written: "The deliverer will come from Zion; he will turn godlessness away from Jacob. And this is my covenant with them when I take away their sins." As far as the gospel is concerned, they are enemies on your account; but as far as election is concerned, they are loved on account of the patriarchs, for God's gifts and his call are irrevocable.

Romans 11:26–29

45

The King James rendition of verse 29 says that "the gifts and calling of God are without repentance." *Without repentance* means "without changing one's mind; without changing direction."

It means that God has not changed His mind.

It means God will never change His mind about the covenant He made with Abraham and his descendants through Isaac and Jacob.

It means God has not changed His mind about their election.

It means God has not changed His mind about their being beloved.

It means God has not changed His mind about His promises to the Jewish people or their calling or their ultimate destiny.

> Just as you who were at one time disobedient to God have now received mercy as a result of their disobedience, so they too have now become disobedient in order that they too may now receive mercy as a result of God's mercy to you.
>
> Romans 11:30–31

What Is Romans Saying?

But Church, we've got a problem. We read Romans 1–8 and are overwhelmed by the tremendous truths they contain. But when we read chapters 9–11, we say all too easily: "These chapters are about the Jews. I'm not a Jew; they're not for me. Oh, thank God, here is chapter 12. I'm safe!"

Dear reader, is this what *you* have been doing? Do you jump from Romans 8 to Romans 12? Have you not heard the Spirit of God speaking through the apostle Paul to all believers:

> I have great sorrow and unceasing anguish in my heart. For I could wish that I myself were cursed and cut off from Christ for the sake of my brothers, those of my own race, the people of Israel. Theirs is the adoption as sons; theirs the divine glory, the covenants, the receiving of the law, the temple worship and the promises. Theirs are the patriarchs, and from them is traced the human ancestry of Christ, who is God over all, forever praised! Amen.
>
> Romans 9:2–5

Does the Bible really say that? Do you believe it?

> Brothers, my heart's desire and prayer to God for the Israelites is that they may be saved. . . . If their transgression means riches for the world, and their loss means riches for the Gentiles, how much greater riches will their fullness bring! I am talking to you Gentiles.
>
> 10:1; 11:12–13

"Their fullness? Impossible! Jesus is only for us. He's not for the Jews. They had their chance and blew it."

> I say then, Have they stumbled that they should fall? God forbid: but rather through their fall salvation is come unto the Gentiles, for to provoke them to jealousy.
>
> 11:11, KJV

"What? Salvation came to the Gentiles so that we would provoke the Jewish people to jealousy? That can't be true. Who put that in the Bible?"

> I would not, brethren, that ye should be ignorant of this mystery, lest ye should be wise in your own conceits; that

47

blindness in part is happened to Israel, until the fulness of the Gentiles be come in.

11:25, KJV

"Blindness in part" has happened to Israel? Yes. But maybe blindness has also happened to the Church.

If their rejection is the reconciliation of the world, what will their acceptance be but life from the dead?

11:15

"This is saying that Jewish people will be reconciled to God one day and we will spend eternity together as co-heirs? How can that be? That's contrary to everything I've been led to believe."

What *have* we been led to believe? Does it go something like this?

"Because the Jewish people rejected Jesus, God has rejected the Jewish people."

"Even the apostle Paul turned away from the Jewish people."

"All God's promises to His chosen people are null and void because they rejected Jesus."

"The blessings God promised the Jewish people now belong to the Church, while to the Jewish people belong His curses."

Church, do you see it? We *do* have a problem. We have made incorrect assumptions about the faithfulness of God to His covenant people. We have not understood that a kind of blindness has happened to Israel "until the full number of the Gentiles has come in" (NIV). What does that mean? What does it mean to you? What does it have to do with the Church?

48

Jesus said that "Jerusalem will be trampled on by the Gentiles until the times of the Gentiles are fulfilled" (Luke 21:24). The phrase *the time of the Gentiles* may be one you haven't thought much about. It refers to the period of history during which Gentiles dominated Europe and the Middle East, including Palestine. Jerusalem itself was governed by Gentiles from the year 70 to the year 1967, when it was restored to Jewish hands. Since then more Jewish people have been receiving Jesus as Messiah and Lord than at any time since the first century. More about this in chapter 9.

Jesus also said,

> "Look at the fig tree and all the trees. When they sprout leaves, you can see for yourselves and know that summer is near. Even so, when you see these things happening, you know that the kingdom of God is near."
>
> Luke 21:29–31

The fig tree—viewed by most scholars as a metaphor for the Jewish people—is blossoming! It's blossoming in the United States and Canada; in South Africa and in England, Scotland, France, Belgium, throughout Europe, Australia and throughout South America. Jewish people are confessing Jesus as their Messiah by the tens of thousands. These messianic Jews, like messianic Gentiles, are receiving the Spirit of life in Messiah Jesus, the grace of God and eternal life.

God's clock is ticking. And it's getting louder. But many of us do not know how to respond to the ticking we hear. We don't know how to act or react in the light of what is happening among Jewish people today. Some might say, "Well, isn't that interesting? Hey, let's talk about our next church supper."

You Really Have to Understand This

I hope you've been able to see in this chapter that many of us in the Church are ignorant of God's never-ending covenant with the Jewish people. I also hope you can see how our incorrect assumptions have affected our relationships with Jewish people, both inside and outside the Church.

It's time for us to remove our self-imposed denominational and theological blinders and face biblical facts. While many refer to the Church as "spiritual Israel," it is not true that all the promises made to the physical descendants of Abraham, Isaac and Jacob now belong to the Church, while His curses belong only to Israel. "God is not a man, that He should lie" (Numbers 23:19). "The gifts and calling of God are without repentance" (Romans 11:29, KJV). He has not changed His mind. And He wants His Church to break free from her "conceits" and realize what time it is. Jesus is challenging us to get on with His work, because He is coming soon.

To prepare us to do that, I invite you to take a walk with me. Let's walk together through Church history and consider how the attitude of the Church toward the Jewish people was formed.

4

Let's Look at Church History

I told you in chapter 1 about my astonishment, after Judy challenged me to read the Bible for myself, that two thousand years ago Jesus was only for the Jewish people and not for the Gentiles, while today—at least in the minds of many—He is only for the Gentiles and not for the Jews.

I marveled then and still marvel: How could this have happened? How *did* it happen? And why?

If you are a Gentile Christian, please believe that my purpose in addressing these questions is not to plant a guilt trip on you. Rather, I want to provide background information that will give you a clearer understanding of why the words *Christ, cross* and *Christian* affect so many Jewish people the way they do. As you gain understanding, you will realize just how far the Church—both her leaders and her members—have strayed from God's will.

51

To make our walk manageable, I will not try to itemize two thousand years of Church history. Instead I will guide you to some of the major foundations of the strong anti-Semitism that developed within the Church over the centuries. I will also provide a panoramic view of the anti-Semitic actions perpetrated by the Church that flowed from those attitudes. Then, in the next chapter, I will address what I consider the fundamental cause of those actions when I raise the question, Why the Holocaust?

Our Walk Begins

To begin our walk through this chapter, I invite you to consider the effectiveness of Jesus' earliest Jewish disciples. Jesus called them apostles—His "sent-forth" ones. As these apostles preached the Gospel to Gentiles as well as Jews, the messianic community grew.

The book of Acts tells us of several problems that surfaced as Gentiles became followers of the Jewish Messiah. Initially the Jewish believers asked, "How can these Gentiles become followers of our Messiah and enter into God's New Covenant with us unless they first become Jewish? Don't they need to be circumcised? Shouldn't they celebrate all the feasts of Israel and observe our traditions?"

The Jewish leaders discussed these questions at length during what came to be known as the Jerusalem Council (see Acts 15). The outcome relieved the Gentile believers: They would *not* have to meet the requirements of the covenant between God and the Jewish nation. Gentile converts (according to Acts 15:20) would have to do only four things:

1. Abstain from food offered previously to idols.
2. Abstain from sexual immorality.

3. Abstain from the meat of strangled animals.
4. Abstain from blood.

Thus freed from having to become Jews—and to fulfill the requirement of circumcision and obey all 613 commandments of the Mosaic Law—more and more Gentiles became believers.

But new questions arose within their midst. Because of the decision of the Jerusalem Council, compounded by Gentile ignorance of the Bible and Jewish history as well as the significance of the Jewishness of Jesus, Jewish traditions and Jewish life, it was difficult for Gentile converts to understand why any Jewish practice should be important to them. The Passover story had little relevance to their own history. And the Jewish calendar was so different from theirs. Even if Jesus did rise from the dead on the third day of Passover, on the eighteenth day of the Hebrew month of Nissan, why did they have to observe the resurrection on that date? Why couldn't they do so on a date more meaningful to and identifiable by them?

In the year 196 C.E. (i.e., of the "Common Era," an easier term for Jewish people to hear than A.D.), a council meeting in Caesarea—which included no Jewish believers—determined that the resurrection of Jesus would be celebrated on a Sunday each year during the Feast of Eshtar, a pagan goddess. In the decades that followed, "Eshtar" Sunday became "Easter" Sunday.

This separation of the resurrection celebration from Passover became more manifest with each succeeding year. Eventually the leaders within the Gentile Church decided that Passover should be eliminated from the Church calendar altogether.

In 325 C.E. an official proclamation was made by the Council of Nicaea (the same council that outlawed a pernicious heresy regarding the nature of Jesus, the God-Man). It declared that Jesus' resurrection was to be observed on Easter Sunday by all believers, Jewish as well as Gentile. A few years later another council held in Antioch decreed that anyone attempting to celebrate the Passover feast on the fifteenth day of Nissan was to be excommunicated.

Such folly! But apparently the Gentiles were sufficiently numerous to confront all Jewish believers with unwarranted arrogance: "We are now the majority. Leave your old ways. Come all the way with us or go back to Judaism. There is no middle ground."

The Church Fathers

As the centuries moved forward, the Church pulled further away from her Jewish roots. Soon she would even deny that she had such roots, and would charge every Jewish person with deicide, since all were allegedly responsible for Christ's death. Forgotten were the many Jews who believed in Jesus as their Messiah and Savior. They were told they would have to suffer for what some of their leaders had done hundreds of years before.

Of critical importance in this pulling away were five Church Fathers—Origen, Justin Martyr, Clement of Alexandria, Tertullian and John Chrysostom—whose theological writings and sermons would affect the relationship of the Church with the Jewish people for almost fifteen hundred years.

Origen

Origen (c. 185–254) may have been most responsible for the early growth of anti-Semitism in the Church. Who was this man? What part did he play in turning the Church from her Jewish roots?

Kenneth Scott Latourette, in his classic *History of Christianity* (Harper & Row, 1975), says this about the second-century teacher from Alexandria:

> Origen was . . . instructed by his father in the Scriptures and in Greek learning. Possessed of an eager mind, he perplexed his father by questions about the deeper meanings which he believed lay behind the words of Holy Writ. . . . A superb teacher, he had a profound influence upon his students. From them and through his writings issued currents which were to help mold Christian thought for generations.

> pp. 148–149

Origen saw in Scripture three levels of meaning:

> First: the common or historical sense which is on the surface for even the simple-minded; second, the soul of the Scriptures which edifies those who perceive it; and third, for the perfect, a meaning hidden under what superficially was repugnant to the conscience or the intellect, but which, discerned, can be expressed by allegory.

> p. 150

Where did the pursuit of hidden meanings lead him? Away from the observance of Jewish holidays.

N. R. M. de Lange in *Origen and the Jews* (Cambridge University Press, 1976), states Origen's position. Since the destruction of the Temple made it impossible for Jews to observe Passover there, as prescribed in Deuteronomy 16:5–6, a literal observance of Passover was therefore impossible—and there remained no reason to celebrate other Jewish festivals either.

As far as the death of Jesus, writes de Lange,

Origen stressed that the culprit was not Pontius Pilate, but the Jewish people, and that the whole of this people had been punished for the crime by being crushed in war and scattered all over the world.

p. 79

Ultimately Origen taught, as a result of his allegorical understanding of Scripture, that since the Jews had rejected Jesus, they had forever forfeited all the rights they had under their covenant with God.

Crucial to [Origen's] whole argument is the paradox that Jews and Gentiles suffer a reversal of roles. The historical Israelites cease to be Israelites, while the believers from the Gentiles become the New Israel. This involves a redefinition of Israel. . . . The figure of Jacob is . . . completely reidentified, with dramatic consequences for the traditional biblical exegesis. Jewish tradition had long identified Esau with the enemies of Israel, and derived satisfaction from the promise that Jacob would prevail over them. Since Jacob now stands for the Church, Esau, the older brother, will represent the Jews. . . . As Origen says, . . . "The closeness of God has been removed from them and transferred to the Church of Christ."

pp. 80–82

That's what Origen believed. But what had God declared? Recall His covenant from Jeremiah 31 (which we looked at, in part, in chapter 2):

This is what the LORD says, he who appoints the sun to shine by day, who decrees the moon and stars to shine by night, who stirs up the sea so that its waves roar— the LORD Almighty is his name: "Only if these decrees vanish from my sight," declares the LORD, "will the descendants of Israel ever cease to be a nation before me." This is what the LORD says: "Only if the heavens above can be

56

measured and the foundations of the earth below be searched out will I reject all the descendants of Israel because of all they have done," declares the LORD.

verses 35–37

Think about the timelessness of this covenant. Then think about the philosophy of Origen—a point of view that actually contradicts Scripture. Origen was teaching that despite the promises of God, despite God's blood covenant commitment to the descendants of Abraham, Isaac and Jacob, and despite the apostle Paul's clear statements in Romans 9–11 about God's future plan for the Jewish people, *God's promises are not to be taken literally but rather allegorized!* The Church would now take Israel's place in the heart of God. Israel as a people no longer mattered to God because she had rejected her Messiah.

And if she no longer mattered to God, individual Jews no longer mattered to Him either. Again from N. R. M. de Lange's *Origen and the Jews*:

He lost no opportunity in his sermons to attack Jewish literalism, and his powerful invective no doubt made its contribution to the later tragic persecution of Jews by Christians.

p. 135

It is important to see what grew from the philosophical seed of Origen's teaching on the Jewish people. From the mountaintop perspective of time, we can see that it produced not a small flowering plant, not a tree, but a wild vine that grew in all directions. Here it burrowed underground as it spread. There it grew into a huge tree, then a forest. Soon there was no containing it; it covered the whole earth. And those who should have known it was not a godly vine were blinded by its flowers even as they were poisoned by its corrupt fruit.

Despite God's warning about what will happen to those who curse the Jewish people (see Genesis 12:3), Origen's teaching that the Jews were unrepentant Christ-killers who had been replaced in the heart of God produced greater and greater hatred for them. It spread from theologian to theologian, from teacher to teacher, from pastor to pastor, from church member to church member, from pagan to pagan. Watch the pattern emerge as you read on.

Justin Martyr

Justin Martyr, another teacher writing in the second century, also saw God's covenant with the Jews as replaced by His covenant with the Church. Lee Martin McDonald, contributing to a compilation entitled *Antisemitism and Early Christianity* (Fortress, 1993), points out that, to Justin,

> Christians had become "the true spiritual Israel" because the Jews had despised and forsaken the law of God and God's holy covenant and had hardened their hearts, refusing to see and perceive the will of God given to them through the prophets.

p. 223

Tertullian

The prominent Latin writer Tertullian from Carthage, North Africa, who died around 230 C.E., was not soon to be outdone in his condemnation of the Jewish people. Lee Martin McDonald quotes him from *Adversus Judaeos 13* as saying that as a result of the Jews' rejection of Christ, "God's grace desisted [from working] among them."

Clement of Alexandria

At the end of the second century, when the Christian Church was beginning to dehumanize Jewish people and institutions, Clement of Alexandria sounded the same theme: The Church has replaced Israel in God's affections.

This convert from paganism also taught (according to McDonald in *Antisemitism and Early Christianity*) that the Scriptures had become the sole possession of the Christians because only they can properly understand them, and because the Scriptures are fulfilled only in Christ.

John Chrysostom

Bishop John Chrysostom rose to prominence in the fourth century as an eloquent preacher of truth and love. His very name, *Chrysostom*, means "golden-mouthed." John became the bishop of Constantinople and was esteemed as one of the greatest of the Church Fathers.

But he gained recognition for something else. Early in the fifth century, he preached eight "Sermons Against the Jews" at Antioch. These, observes Paul Johnson in his acclaimed *History of the Jews* (Harper & Row, 1987),

> became the pattern for anti-Jewish tirades, making the fullest possible use (and misuse) of key passages in the gospels of St Matthew and John. Thus a specifically Christian anti-Semitism, presenting the Jews as murderers of Christ, was grafted on to the seething mass of pagan smears and rumours, and Jewish communities were now at risk in every Christian city.

> p. 165

Chrysostom's view of the synagogue, quoted by Malcolm Hay in *The Roots of Christian Anti-Semitism* (Liberty Press, 1981), reveals his hatred:

The synagogue was . . . a criminal assembly of Jews . . . in a place of meeting for the assassins of Christ . . . a house worse than a drinking shop . . . a den of thieves; a house of ill fame, a dwelling of iniquity, the refuge of devils, a gulf and abyss of perdition.

p. 28

Malcolm Hay goes on to comment:

The violence of the language used by St. John Chrysostom in his homilies against the Jews has never been exceeded by any preacher whose sermons have been recorded. . . . These homilies, moreover, were used for centuries, in schools and in seminaries where priests were taught to preach, with St. John Chrysostom as their model—where priests were taught to hate, with St. John Chrysostom as their model.

p. 27

Venom in the golden mouth of Chrysostom was spewed for many generations through the mouths of his followers.

The Crusades

During the long, dark years of the Middle Ages, the ideas of Origen, Justin Martyr, Tertullian, Clement of Alexandria and John Chrysostom were reflected in the teachings of other leaders in the Church. As a result, Jews were frequently given the option of baptism or expulsion, baptism or torture, baptism or death.

In his book *A History of the Jews* (Knopf, 1971), Abram L. Sachar, noted historian and founding president of Brandeis University, helps us better to visualize what took place over the centuries and how the ideas we have been looking at affected the Jewish people. From France at the end of the eleventh century:

> As the influence of the clergy widened and the Church orders gained in power, local persecutions became common. An envenomed sermon by an ignorant fanatic often impelled the simple folks of a community to burn down synagogues and homes and to lay violent hands on the Jews. It became an annual custom in Beziers, in the week between Palm Sunday and Easter Monday, when the priests described the sufferings of Jesus, to pelt the Jews with mud and stones whenever they appeared. In Toulouse, the count in the city had the right to slap the face of the Jewish leader on Good Friday.
>
> p. 186

Sachar goes on to explain that soon nearly all of Europe "knelt at [the] feet" of Pope Gregory II, who mandated severe restrictions against Jews and outlawed their public employment.

About the year 1100 came the Crusades, the military expeditions undertaken by European Christians to recover the Holy Land from the Muslims. Ostensibly religious motives launched the Crusades, but the countless men, women and children who were tortured and killed in those years soon gave the lie to those religious motives.

How did the Crusades impact the Jewish people? Astonishingly! And very quickly. Chaim Potok in his book *Wanderings* (Fawcett Crest, 1978) writes:

> As the peasant host made its way southward it began to attack and pillage the Jewish communities along the Rhine. About eight hundred Jews were killed in Worms after days of heavy fighting. More than a thousand died in Mainz. They were buried in ditches. In Cologne the synagogue was destroyed. . . . The peasant mob continued

southward, offering Jews apostasy or death. Most chose martyrdom.

p. 409

So the carnage was multiplied. Try to imagine the fear the Jewish people experienced during the early decades of the Crusades. Can you fathom what it was like to have to search everyone's eyes to gauge his or her level of hate? Can you sense what it was like to live in fear for your life? What would you tell your children when they wanted to go out to play, not knowing if the Crusaders had left town or whether a new attack might soon be under way? How much would *you* have to do with the "Christians"?

As time passed and no other attacks came, your fear would begin to dissipate. Life would appear normal again. Then, like an ear-splitting burst of thunder, another Crusade would destroy your peace—one even worse than the last one.

Sachar continues:

> It seemed as if the end would never come. Every defeat of the crusaders brought the wrath of failure; every victory brought the assaults of pride. . . . The crusades are a turning point in Jewish history. They mark the end of settled Jewish communal life in Europe, the beginning of intense race-aversions. They usher in the Jewish caricature who stalked through Europe, the pariah with bent back and hunted look and obsequious manner, bitter over his yesterdays and fearful of his tomorrows.

pp. 191–192

For Jewish people, the arrival of the thirteenth century offered little relief. Indeed, the persecution intensified. Jews were degraded in body and spirit. They were required, as a precursor of what would happen in Nazi Germany, to wear badges of shame. In city after city throughout Europe, they were humiliated and degraded. Soon they were expelled from countries in which, as Sachar points out, they had lived longer than those expelling them.

Again I ask you to imagine yourself as a Jew living in those years. Picture yourself trying to explain to your children why the "Christians" hate them. Think how you would feel pelted with stones or rotten vegetables by laughing "Christian" children as you walked down the street wearing the mark of a Jew.

Or try to imagine how you would respond when you learn that your grandparents and parents had been trapped in the synagogue when it was torched and burned by the Crusaders. Your loved ones and hundreds of other Jews who were praying in the synagogue for God's protection are now ashes in the dust of the ghetto. How do you respond to this news? What happens inside of you? How do you handle your anger? What do you do with your shame? What happens to your self-respect? To whom do you turn for comfort? What do you say to comfort others? Feel the humiliation. Taste the rejection. Smell the fear.

Again from Sachar:

As decade followed decade in the thirteenth century, the world began to take for granted that Jews were not men, but tools to be used and thrown away or targets to be fired upon in any contingency—when crops were bad or wine mounted to the head, when an Easter sermon struck home too literally or a noble's purse was pinched.

p. 197

What had these Jews done to deserve this fate? Nothing. They were simply Jews.

Chaim Potok recounts in *Wanderings* that five thousand Jews of England were expelled in 1290 and taken in by the dukes of central France. The Jews of France were expelled repeatedly, then allowed to return, until they were banished for good in 1394. Potok reminds us of the conviction of Pope Innocent III that "the guilt of the Jews for the crucifixion of Jesus consigned them to perpetual servitude, and, like Cain, they were to be wanderers and fugitives."

The Inquisition

Some say that Jews arrived in Spain as early as Nebuchadnezzar's day. Others purport that the major influx of Jews to Spain took place after the failure of the second Jewish uprising against Rome in the year 135 C.E. Whatever the date of their arrival, it is important to know that the history of Spain was enmeshed to a great extent with the history of the Jewish people.

Felipe Torroba Bernaldo de Aquiros, in his book *The Spanish Jews* (S. A. Paseo Onesimo Redondo, 1972), describes how wonderful many of those centuries were for the Jews. Spain prospered, too—in part because of them. But the Jewish population grew so large that some felt something had to be done. De Aquiros describes a few of the actions taken against the Jews in the fourteenth century to punish them and overturn their success:

> The Council of Illiberis . . . decreed that they should live apart from the Hispano-Romans and forbade their marriage to Christian girls, unless they were converted. A strict separation was also decreed between the Hispano-Roman race and the Semitic one, which was considered as impure. An attempt was made to prevent all kinds of intercommunication with its members, and it was even considered that the blessings of fields or crops, or any kind of goods, by the rabbis would attract all types of

calamities. It was forbidden for a Christian to share the table with a Jew, and the Christian who took a Jewess as his lover was anathematized.

p. 14

Chaim Potok writes of the next few decades:

The fortunes of the Jews of Spain rose and fell with the needs and whims of kings. . . . In 1412 the government of Castile ordered Jews to inhabit separate quarters in towns and villages. They were to be distinguished from Christians by growing their hair and beards. There were about thirty thousand Jewish families in Castile at the time. . . . The inquisition intensified its work, investigating, judging, consigning people to the stake.

pp. 422–423

How delicately put! Potok goes on to recount:

On March 31, 1492, an edict of expulsion directed against the Jews was signed in Granada. On May 1 of that year, Spain began to expel all Jews who would not accept Christianity. About 170,000 left the land. They went wandering through Europe, Portugal, North Africa, Turkey. Tens of thousands accepted baptism. The last Jew left Spain on July 31, 1492. Spain was officially empty of Jews. Pope Innocent III had triumphed. All the Jews were wanderers, lost in a vast, enchanted world.

p. 423

Many Jews (as we have seen) did not leave Spain in 1492. To save their lives and the lives of their families, they converted to Catholicism. Many of these, who became known as the Marranos, continued to practice Judaism in secret. Cecil Roth in *A History of the Marranos* (Shocken, 1974) explains that they were watched carefully to see if they were practicing "heresy." Heretical practices included failure to eat pork; failure to work on Saturday; failure to wear one's best clothes on Sunday; keeping the biblical feasts; observing any Jewish customs of any kind; saying any Jewish prayers; preparing food according to Jewish law; associating with non-baptized Jews; and intermarriage of children of Marrano families with children of other Marrano families.

p. 77

And if someone was caught?

Violators, or frequently those merely accused of being violators, would have their property confiscated. They would be subjected to harsh confinement and horrible torture, leading to mock trials, degradation and often death at the stake. If those sentenced to die would renounce their "heresies" and publicly confess the Faith, then the Church would show them mercy: they would be strangled and then put to the flame, burned dead instead of alive.

p. 32

During the Spanish Inquisition, between thirty thousand and fifty thousand Marranos were burned at the stake.

Before we leave this section, I want to remind you again of the multiplied thousands of Jews forced to flee from their homes and their countries. Try to visualize the confusion that gripped their hearts. They weren't sure where they would go. They weren't sure they would be safe on the journey.

See the thousands who walk in one direction and other thousands who walk in another. Day after day they walk, hoping to find safety. See the fortunate ones traveling in carts. Picture the very old and the very young. Picture those who cannot walk any farther and who fall to the ground in despair. Hear them weeping. See the fear in the eyes of the children. Shake your head in shock at the injustice of it. Let gall burn in your throat. Let your eyes fill with tears. And then weep with me over this horrible tragedy.

The Arrival of Martin Luther

Inquisitions against Jewish people continued for more than seven hundred years, from the twelfth to the nineteenth centuries, throughout Western and Central Europe. In all those centuries, Jews were blamed for the underlying illness of European society. Imagine how *you* would feel about the "Christians" who did this to your people.

In 1517 a Roman Catholic monk, Martin Luther, challenged the Church in what became the Protestant Reformation. In 1523, two years after his excommunication, he broke from its ingrained position concerning the Jewish people:

> Perhaps I will attract some of the Jews to the Christian faith. For our fools—the popes, bishops, sophists, and monks—the course blockheads! have until this time so treated the Jews that if I had been a Jew and had seen such idiots and blockheads ruling and teaching the Christian religion, I would rather have been a sow than a Christian. For they have dealt with the Jews as if they were dogs and not human beings.
>
> *Disputation and Dialogue: Readings in the Jewish-Christian Encounter* (Ktav/Anti-Defamation League of B'nai B'rith, 1975), p. 33

Unfortunately Luther did not maintain this opinion. Toward the end of his life, frustrated because more Jewish people had not professed faith in Jesus Christ, the Reformer published a widely circulated pamphlet in 1543,

Von den Juden und Ihren Lügen ("On the Jews and Their Lies"), which Paul Johnson in *A History of the Jews* terms "the first work of modern anti-Semitism, and a giant step forward on the road to the Holocaust."

Luther's arguments against the Jews in this pamphlet are summarized by Will Durant in his *The Story of Civilization*, Volume 6, *The Reformation* (MJF Books, 1957):

> . . . that they had refused to accept Christ as God, that their age-long sufferings proved God's hatred of them, that they were intruders in Christian lands, that they were insolent in their usurious prosperity, that the Talmud sanctioned the deception, robbery, and killing of Christians, that they poisoned springs and wells, and murdered Christian children to use their blood in Jewish rituals.
>
> p. 727

Here, according to Paul Johnson, were Luther's remedies:

> 'First,' he urged, 'their synagogues should be set on fire, and whatever is left should be buried in dirt so that no one may ever be able to see a stone or cinder of it.' Jewish prayer-books should be destroyed and rabbis forbidden to preach. Then the Jewish people should be dealt with, their homes 'smashed and destroyed' and their inmates 'put under one roof or in a stable like gypsies, to teach them they are not master in our land.' Jews should be banned from the roads and markets, their property seized and then these 'poisonous envenomed worms' should be drafted into forced labour and made to earn their bread 'by the sweat of their noses.'
>
> p. 242

Durant points out that Luther ultimately advised giving "all Jews a choice between Christianity and having their tongues torn out."

Note the observation of Raul Hilberg, a scholar of the Holocaust, in *The Destruction of the European Jews* (Holmes & Meier, 1985):

> Luther's ideas were shared by others in his century and the mode of his expression was the style of his times. His work is cited here only because he was the towering figure in the development of German thought, and the writing of such a man is not to be forgotten in the unearthing of so crucial a conceptualization as this.

p. 15

How, then, shall we summarize the period from 1300 to 1700? In Hilberg's words, "The Jews of England, France, Germany, Spain, Bohemia and Italy were presented with ultimatums that gave them no choice but one: conversion or expulsion."

As if in response to Luther's urging, laws were made to further segregate and punish the Jews. Max I. Dimont in *Jews, God and History* refers to a "crazy quilt of anti-Jewish laws" passed between the sixteenth and the eighteenth centuries. These laws

> . . . not only were aimed at isolating the Jews more and more from the Christians, but were also designed to make them objects of scorn and derision, to deprive them of any symbol of dignity, and to make people forget their former learning. These new laws tended to make Jewish persecutions more and more abstract until the very reason for their origin became obscured, then forgotten, until only a dehumanized symbol of a denigrated Jew remained. New generations of Christians who did not know of the proud, learned Jew of other days, saw only a queerly dressed ghetto Jew, wearing a black caftan, a yellow patch of ignominy, a ridiculous peaked hat—an object of derision and scorn.

p. 234

Over the next two hundred years, theologians embroidered their own initials into the tapestry Luther had woven. Pater Constant, a doctor of two faculties writing in 1897, expounded on one of the prohibitions between Christians and Jews: A Christian woman must not serve as wet nurse for a Jewish child. Here he is quoted by Count Heinrich Coudenhove-Kalergi in *Anti-Semitism throughout the Ages* (Greenwood Press, 1972):

> The body of the Christian, so religion teaches us, is the temple of the Holy Ghost. The same religion also teaches us that the body which has not been washed and cleansed in baptism remains the abode of the devil. To establish those intimate relations which exist in the case of a nursing between the body of a Christian woman and a Jewish child, appeared to the Church to be an outrage, that of bringing the devil into contact with the Holy Ghost.

> p. 92

Hitler

Adolf Hitler echoed the ostensibly theological basis of anti-Semitism in *Mein Kampf* when he wrote, "Today, I believe that I am acting in accordance with the Almighty Creator: by defending myself against the Jew, I am fighting for the work of the Lord."

The Encyclopedia Judaica (Keter Publishing House, 1973) quotes Hitler from January 30, 1939:

> In my life I have often been a prophet, and most of the time I have been laughed at. During the period of my struggle for power, it was the Jewish people that received with laughter my prophecies that someday I would take over the leadership of the state and thereby of the whole people, and that I would among other things also solve

the Jewish problem. Today I want to be a prophet once more: if international-finance Jewry inside and outside of Europe should succeed once more in plunging nations into another world war, the consequence will not be the Bolshevization of the earth and thereby the victory of Jewry, but the annihilation of the Jewish race in Europe.

p. 852

Extreme as Hitler's views were, Raul Hilberg purports in *The Destruction of the European Jews* that the German Nazis "did not discard the past; they built upon it":

The missionaries of Christianity had said in effect: You have no right to live among us as Jews. The secular rulers who followed had proclaimed: You have no right to live among us. The German Nazis at last decreed: You have no right to live.

pp. 8–9

Pause for Some Perspective

How unbelievably horrible these aspects of history are! How far from the will of God for His Church and for the Jewish people! So why have I reviewed these philosophies and events with you? Because few people today know anything about these shameful annals of the Church.

I have not sought in this chapter to recount individual acts of hatred that adherents of the Church inflicted on the Jewish people. Rather, I have tried to assess the foundation for that hatred in the teachings of early theologians who based their writings on human ideas rather than on the Word of God.

As if to emphasize this emerging phenomenon, Raul Hilberg writes:

71

Since the fourth century after Christ there have been three anti-Jewish policies: conversion, expulsion and annihilation. The second appeared as an alternative to the first, and the third emerged as an alternative to the second.

p. 8

We have seen in this chapter that what amounted to the worst kind of genocide in the twentieth century actually began in the first and second centuries, in the hearts and minds of Gentile followers of the Messiah, as ignorance about their Jewish roots. The visual symbols of that hatred—the cross, the crucifix bearing an Aryan Christ, the church building itself, the barbed wire of the Holocaust—have left their imprints on the conscious and subconscious memories of the Jewish people. Is it any wonder that these symbols often strike fear into Jewish hearts today?

Surely you can see that for most of the past two thousand years, the reality of Jesus' Messiahship has not been the subject separating Jews from Christians. Nor has the Son of God been the subject of discussion. The Jewish people, instead of hearing about and experiencing Him, have heard about and experienced every imaginable evil act that one person can inflict on another. And these were done in the name of Jesus!

Where was the Prince of Peace then? Where was the Jewish Messiah over those centuries? Where was the love of God for His chosen people?

Do you hear the pain in these questions? But pause for just a moment, because our story is not quite finished. Yet to be considered is the "final solution" to the Jewish question—one of the most heinous and inexplicable events of world history.

Still, I will try to explain it.

Why the Holocaust?

In the last four chapters I set out to provide background information you need in order to better understand the present mindset of both the Jewish people and the Church. In the last chapter I listed some of the horrible things done to the Jewish people of the world in the name of Christ. It is inevitable to realize, in light of history, how far the Church strayed from God's plan to restore the Jewish people to Himself. Century after century of persecution by Christians did little to attract Jewish people to the message of the Gospel. And then the "final solution" was upon them.

Where was the Church when six million Jews were exterminated to accomplish Hitler's master plan?

Many Jewish people believe Adolf Hitler could never have succeeded with his plan to destroy the Jewish people without the help of the Christian Democratic Party in

73

Germany. They also believe he had the help of the Christians of the world who let the Holocaust happen because of their indifference to the plight of the Jews. Jews still cannot cope with the refusal of Pope Pius XII (1896–1958) to issue any public condemnation of National Socialism, anti-Semitism or the deliberate slaughter of the majority of European Jewry. Is it any wonder that, in the eyes of many Jewish people, the Church participated in the Holocaust by her silence?

Then there is the question, Where was God during the Holocaust? This is one of the most somber and unanswerable questions a Jewish person can ask. How could God allow this tragedy to happen to us?

Some Kids I Remember from Wartime

I was only sixteen years old in 1940 and did not understand the depth of what was going on in Nazi Germany. But I do remember the Jewish kids I knew who had been raised there. Their parents got them out in the years just before World War II while it was still possible to do so.

I will never forget some of the stories they told about what they and their parents went through in order to get out of Germany.

Teddy

When I met Teddy, my mother, father, older brother Sam, sister Dorris and I were living in the four-room apartment I mentioned in chapter 1—with one bathroom and no elevator!—on the top floor of a four-story apartment building in Brooklyn. Teddy and his family lived a few buildings away.

Teddy was tall and thin with huge blue eyes. He had been raised in Berlin, where his father had been a famous psychiatrist. As we came to know each other, Teddy told me what his life had been like in Berlin just two years before.

His family had lived in a very large house on the edge of the German capital. His sister, younger brother and he each had separate bedrooms. His parents owned two cars. They also had a gardener and housekeeper. To me, living where I lived, without even one car in the family, this sounded like a fairy tale.

Then Teddy explained how lucky he and his family were to get out of Germany, even if they had to live in a small apartment. He described how his father had come home one day and called the entire family together. After trying for many months, he had finally received permission to leave Germany and come to America. They were to leave by ship in six days. Each member of the family was pledged to silence, telling no one they would be leaving Germany.

With tears in his eyes, Teddy recounted that they just walked away from their home and possessions in order to escape the anti-Semitism and death that awaited them if they did not get out of Germany. Each of them could take only one suitcase on the journey. He also told us of his grandparents, aunts, uncles and cousins who did not get out of Germany and from whom they had heard nothing in more than a year. They feared that the worst had happened.

Though Teddy's father had been a prominent psychiatrist in Berlin, he was grateful for his present job as an orderly in a local hospital, and for the opportunity he now had to go to school.

What crime had been committed to cause such a transformation in the lives of this entire family? Only one. They were Jews.

I was open-mouthed as Teddy told his story. *Why did this happen?* I wondered. *Why isn't someone doing some-*

*thing about this? What do these Christians want from us?
Why don't they leave us alone?*

Trudy

These were questions Trudy asked, too. She and her
family were from Stuttgart. I met her when she joined our
eighth-grade class. Although Trudy was more a friend of
Ethel's than mine, when we were together she often spoke
of their lives in Stuttgart.

Her father, a manufacturer, had employed hundreds
of people in his factory. Her parents, highly respected and
affluent, lived in a large home and had several servants.
But her father could read the handwriting on the wall,
and soon after Kristallnacht—the night of November
9–10, 1938, when the Nazis smashed the windows of thousands of stores owned by Jewish merchants, set fire to
many synagogues, lighted huge public bonfires and
burned books written by Jewish authors—he knew he
had to get his family out. It took a great deal of money and
many months to arrange, but Trudy and her entire family were able to escape to America.

What crime had they committed? They were Jews.

Stella

Stella's family was not quite as lucky as Teddy's or
Trudy's. Not too many weeks after all Jews were required
to wear armbands with Stars of David on them, her father
managed to send his children abroad. Stella's older sister was sent to London to live with relatives there, but
Stella came to the United States to stay with relatives who
lived on our block.

Stella's father never thought the Nazis would bother him
because he was the president of a large bank in Berlin. Since

he knew many of the political higher-ups and did business with them, he felt fairly secure. And one of those friends did help him—but not in the way he expected. One day the friend called to warn him that the Storm Troopers were coming for him. What did Stella's father do with this information? He closed the door to his office and shot himself.

Stella's mother, we learned later, was taken to a concentration camp, where she died.

Why did Stella's parents have to die? They were Jews.

Lisa

Not all German Jews had wonderful jobs and lots of money. Lisa's story was closer to the norm. There was no way her father could accumulate the large amount of money needed to buy the family out of Germany and get them to America. But family members in New York got together and arranged for Lisa and her younger sister, Freda (short for Fredericka), to join them.

When I first saw Lisa, I noticed how pretty she was. She was about 5' 2" with blond hair and big blue eyes. I particularly noticed her hair and eyes because few of the girls in our crowd were blonde. Lisa and Freda were talented violinists who were not always able to go out with the kids because they had to practice.

Their cousins loved and provided for Lisa and Freda, but they were terribly homesick for their parents and other relatives. None of the other family members made it. They all were liquidated at Buchenwald.

Their crime? They were Jews.

Uncle Sam, Here I Come

Anti-Semitism did not exist only in Germany. Its seeds had sprouted in America as well. I remember hearing

President Franklin D. Roosevelt vilified because, the lie went, he had changed his name from Rosenfeld. Jews could not live in certain neighborhoods. They could not be employed in certain professions. They could not get into certain schools. And the quota system was the rule in almost all colleges and universities: They would accept only so many Jews, so many blacks, so many Asians.

When Ethel was studying at Brooklyn College in 1944, she was one of five honor students sent from the school, at the request of a local manufacturer of wartime materials, for part-time work at the factory. One student was black, one was Asian, two were Jews and one was a white, Anglo-Saxon Protestant (WASP). After they filled out their applications for employment, a personnel worker explained that the company did not hire Jews, blacks or Asians. Only the WASP would be hired.

"Oh, no," said the young man who had been accepted. "If my friends aren't good enough to work here, I'm too good to work here."

And they all left together.

I joined the U.S. Army on February 9, 1943, angry about what was going on in Germany and ready to do my part to rid our world of Hitler and his Nazi followers. In December 1944 I was relieved to learn that my outfit would not be going to the Far East but to Europe. A few months later, on April 4, 1945, we crossed the Rhine River into Germany, just days after the Infantry. As we approached Frankfurt am Main, our truck stopped so that we could see what remained of the city. It was a huge pile of rubble. We were delighted to see what our Air Force and artillery had accomplished.

I never visited any of the concentration camps but heard the horror stories over and over. Soldiers who had been there told us about the death camps where Jewish bodies had been burned by the hundreds of thousands.

Rumors also flew about the horrible smell of burned flesh in the camps. Then I heard about the mass graves where dead Jews who had been gassed were covered with lime and left to rot.

Later our armed forces newspaper, *Stars and Stripes*, ran pictures of the camps being liberated. I saw the faces of the Jews who survived. They looked like skeletons—big eyes, protruding cheekbones, hollowed-out cheeks. As they were liberated from the camps, they looked emaciated in their striped prison uniforms, dazed, overwhelmed.

Almost before we knew it, Germany surrendered. It was over. We had destroyed the Nazi monster.

How happy I was later when the full story of the atrocities emerged through the Nuremberg trials of 1945–1946 and was published worldwide. Many Nazi criminals were convicted of crimes they had committed and some were executed.

But each succeeding year, as I pursued my education and set out to build a career, took me further and further from the Holocaust.

Remembrances

Then, in May 1973, after I had become successful in business, Ethel and I went to Israel to celebrate our 25th wedding anniversary, as well as the 25th anniversary of the founding of the State of Israel. It was our first trip there.

At Y'ad Vashem, the Holocaust memorial in Jerusalem, I stood in front of life-sized pictures of Jews huddled together in concentration camps behind barbed wire. Each picture seemed to reflect the same faces. Their eyes looked so empty. Their frames were so gaunt that their prison clothes hung on their bones—hundreds of men and women who looked just like me. They could have been my cousins! They looked bewildered and alone, even as they grouped before their overstuffed and smiling guards.

I wept as I looked at those pictures. I wept as I saw other pictures of bulldozers pushing Jewish bodies into mass graves, and pictures of the gas chambers and ovens where so many Jews had been cremated. I wept as I saw lampshades made from Jewish skin, and collections of gold taken from Jewish teeth.

In many ways my first visit to Y'ad Vashem was a mind-blowing flashback to 1945. Here were the faces I had not seen then, even worse than I had imagined them to be.

But I did not weep only for those who had been killed so savagely. I wept for myself, too, because there but for the grace of God was I. After all, I am a Jew, too.

I made frequent visits to Y'ad Vashem after I became a believer and the pastor of an interdenominational congregation made up of Jewish and Gentile believers. Periodically I led tours to Israel and always took the members to Y'ad Vashem.

The first time I went into the children's exhibit, I wasn't sure what I would see, but I had heard that I must not miss it.

The auditorium we entered was very large on the outside and almost totally dark on the inside. We were told to hold onto the rail so that we would not lose our way. The first thing I heard was the music—a dirge in a minor key. Then there were the lights—hundreds and even thousands of little lights sparkling all around the exhibit. Then I became aware of what I was hearing. Names were being read. Jewish names. Names of Jewish children who had been killed by the Nazis, just because they were Jewish.

As we made our way through the exhibit, holding onto the railing, I was glad we were in almost total darkness and that no one could see my tears. It was an awesome experience, something I will never forget.

Some years later I made my first visit to one of the most remarkable facilities to be created in recent years, the United States Holocaust Memorial Museum in Washington, D.C. After going through security, I lined up with a group in front of one of the elevators that would take us to the starting point for the exhibit. An identification card was given to each of us that showed the seal of the United States of America with these words above it: *For the dead and the living we must bear witness.* Inside my ID card was the picture and story of a man who lived during the Holocaust.

That did it. Once again I was caught up in the reality of the horrible days of Hitler. The elevator that took us to the top floor was larger than most. As it filled with people, I couldn't help thinking of all the Jewish people herded into boxcars. From the moment the steel doors shut behind me, I had the feeling I was going backward in time.

When the elevator doors opened, the first thing I saw was a twelve-foot-by-twelve-foot black-and-white photograph of American GIs on Liberation Day looking at the burned bodies of Jewish men, women and children at the Ohrdruff concentration camp in central Germany. Shock was visible on the soldiers' faces, just as it must have been visible on mine. The next picture showed a Jewish man being led out of the prison gates at Buchenwald. Then I paused before a large picture of General Dwight D. Eisenhower next to a statement he had made on April 15, 1945:

> The things I saw beggar description. The visual evidence and the verbal testimony of starvation, cruelty and bes-

81

tiality were overpowering. I made the visit deliberately in order to be in a position to give first-hand evidence of these things if ever, in the future, there was a tendency to charge these allegations merely to propaganda.

The setting of the museum is both somber and depressing. The inside of the building is constructed of steel and brick, evocative of the death camps. Following each section of black-and-white photographs, a TV-type monitor describes a different aspect of what life was like for the Jewish people before and during Hitler's regime. The humiliation and degradation they experienced is almost palpable.

Then there are the testimonies. A little amphitheater shows film clips of Jewish men and women who survived the camps. As they recount their experiences, it is almost as if they are reliving them. My heart was touched by the nobility of these people as they shared their testimonies. As one man said, his burden is that he still remembers so clearly what happened.

One of the exhibits that touched me most deeply showed thousands of men, women and children being lined up at Crematorium II in Auschwitz-Birkenau, with this description:

Victims arrived in Crematorium II through a stairway leading down to the undressing room, which held about 1,000 people. Here SS guards and specially trained inmates told them to surrender their valuables and to undress for a delousing shower. Victims were told to remember where they had left their clothing, and posters on the walls bore slogans such as "Cleanliness Brings Freedom" and "One Louse Can Kill." These were attempts, often successful, to lull the victims into thinking they were to take a hygienic shower.

When the victims had taken off all their clothes, they were herded into an underground gas chamber disguised with false shower heads as a shower room. Women and children, who were usually in the majority, went in first. As soon as the chamber was filled with people, sealed and locked, SS guards poured zyklon-B pellets in through special vents in the roof. The pellets fell to the floor, releasing their deadly gas. Most of the victims died within a few minutes. After about 20 minutes when all were dead, ventilators were turned on to get rid of the poisonous gas.

People stood before this exhibit in stunned silence for what seemed like a very long time.

Focus on the Question *Why?*

In light of all this, can you imagine how I feel each time I go into one of my favorite Jewish supermarkets and see the tattooed numbers on the wrists of men and women who work behind the bakery or deli counter? Or each time I learn of someone actually contending openly that the Holocaust never happened? Or when I hear people say, "Hey, that happened back then. This is today. It's time to forget it!"

It is *not* time to forget it. There will never be a time to forget it.

Many books have been written about the Holocaust that describe the terrible years of Hitler's power and satanic madness. Many have examined the Holocaust from a psychological or sociological viewpoint. But few, to my knowledge, have attempted to explain the Holocaust from a biblical or spiritual perspective. Until we do, we will never be able to understand it fully. (And always we should write the word *mystery* large across the whole Hitlerite period. Demonic forces were involved that are beyond human comprehension.)

Why did the Holocaust happen? Why did the United States remain silent for so long? And England? And the rest of the world? Why did the Pope and the Catholic Church not speak out? Why did the majority of the believers of the world remain silent?

"The Holocaust," some say, "was God's way of punishing the Jews for their rejection of Jesus."

I shudder at that statement. I shudder even more to think that any student of the Bible might think it is true. If it *were* true, why were only the Jews in Europe selected to die? Why not the Jews in America, or in Canada, or in South America? Why not Jews all over the world? Also, why then and not sooner? Why then and not now?

No, that statement is absolutely not true. In fact, nothing could be further from the truth. Recall Jesus praying from the cross, "Father, forgive them; for they know not what they do" (Luke 23:34, KJV). And recall God's present and future plans for the Jewish people as expressed in the book of Romans (which we looked at in chapter 3). Paul asked, "Did God reject his people?" and answered his own question emphatically, "By no means!" (Romans 11:1).

When you reread Romans 11 carefully, you will notice the number of times that future events concerning Israel and the Jewish people are mentioned. You will also notice that in verse 7, Paul declares it was God who deafened their ears and blinded their eyes so they could not hear or see. And you will be reminded of this amazing truth: "I do not want you to be ignorant of this mystery, brothers, so that you may not be conceited: Israel has experienced a hardening in part until the full number of the Gentiles has come in" (verse 25).

The word *hardening* takes us all the way back to the book of Exodus and Moses' efforts to get Pharaoh to let the children of Israel leave Egypt. But God told Moses, "I will harden [Pharaoh's] heart so that he will not let the people go" (Exodus 4:21).

The word *until* in Romans 11:25 is crucial to our understanding of God's intentions concerning the Jewish people. God *does* have a future plan for us. When will it be fully manifest? When "the full number of the Gentiles" has come to faith.

And what will happen then?

All Israel will be saved, as it is written: "The deliverer will come from Zion; he will turn godlessness away from Jacob. And this is my covenant with them when I take away their sins." As far as the gospel is concerned, they are enemies on your account; but as far as election is concerned, they are loved on account of the patriarchs.

verses 26–28

Make sure you grasp Paul's emphasis in these verses: "As far as the gospel is concerned, they are enemies on your account."

He was not saying the Jewish people are *your* enemies. He did not say you are their enemies. He did not say they are God's enemies. He did not say God is their enemy. He said, "As far as the gospel is concerned, they are enemies on your account."

On your account, if you are a Gentile. Because of you.

For what reason and for how long? "Until the full number of the Gentiles has come in."

But Paul also said, "As far as election is concerned, they are loved."

Loved by whom? By almighty God.

Has God changed His mind?

So Who Is to Blame?

Do you see it? God hardened Jewish hearts so that they would not receive Him. He blinded their eyes and deafened their ears. Why? So the Gospel would not bring about an encapsulated sect within Jewish life, but be taken to all the world and become a universal faith.

Well, then, if God loves the Jewish people and did not send the Holocaust to punish them for their rejection of Jesus, why did it happen? Who is to blame?

The Bible teaches that believers do not battle against flesh and blood, but against principalities and powers (see Ephesians 6:12). All too often things in the natural world originated in the spiritual world. Remember, Satan was cast down from heaven because of his rebellion and pride. It was not that he rebelled against the power of God. He envied God's power, of course, but what he really rebelled against was His authority.

Satan still struggles to exalt his own authority above the authority of God, even though Jesus stripped him of his power by the cross (see Colossians 2:15). Continually Satan accuses God before men and women. He accuses men and women before God. And he accuses men and women before one another.

One of the ways Satan tries to accuse God, as we have already seen, is to try to make God out to be a liar. He started doing this with Eve in the Garden. "Did God really say. . . ?" he asked, and then went on to dismiss what God said as not true (see Genesis 3:1, 4–5). He hoped to undermine Eve's confidence in the integrity of God. And he has been accusing God before men and women ever since.

We Jewish people should be especially on guard against any temptation to doubt what God has said in the Bible, particularly about us as a people. When we examine the promises God made to Abraham and his descendants (see Genesis 12:1–3; 17:1–7), we find that He has made tremendous commitments to the Jewish people— the sort of commitments that will last forever.

But if Satan could hold up to ridicule even one of God's promises, he would cause people to think God had lied and should not be trusted.

Reviewing God's Promises

As we saw in chapter 2, God made other very specific promises to the Jewish people. The first had to do with the New Covenant. The second had to do with the survival of the Jewish people as a nation before God. Let's reread these promises before we consider Satan's response to them.

First, the New Covenant:

> "The time is coming," declares the LORD, "when I will make a new covenant with the house of Israel and with the house of Judah. It will not be like the covenant I made with their forefathers when I took them by the hand to lead them out of Egypt, because they broke my covenant, though I was a husband to them," declares the LORD.
>
> "This is the covenant I will make with the house of Israel after that time," declares the LORD. "I will put my law in their minds and write it on their hearts. I will be their God, and they will be my people. No longer will a man teach his neighbor, or a man his brother, saying, 'Know the LORD,' because they will all know me, from the least of them to the greatest," declares the LORD. "For I will forgive their wickedness and will remember their sins no more."
>
> Jeremiah 31:31–34

Although Satan did everything he could do to prevent God's promise of the New Covenant from being fulfilled, God fulfilled it wonderfully and completely. After Jesus was resurrected, He bestowed the Holy Spirit on His disciples that they might keep His Law and become a people who would know and obey Him (see Luke 22:20; 1 Corinthians 11:25; Hebrews 8:8–10; 10:16–17).

Now review these two specific promises regarding the survival of the Jewish people as a nation before God:

> This is what the LORD says, he who appoints the sun to shine by day, who decrees the moon and stars to shine by night, who stirs up the sea so that its waves roar—the LORD Almighty is his name: "Only if these decrees vanish from my sight," declares the LORD, "will the descendants of Israel ever cease to be a nation before me."
>
> This is what the LORD says: "Only if the heavens above can be measured and the foundations of the earth below be searched out will I reject all the descendants of Israel because of all they have done," declares the LORD.
>
> Jeremiah 31:35–37

Do you believe God will fulfill these two promises—that Israel will endure as long as the sun, moon and stars shine; and that there will always be a remnant of Israel remaining despite what they might do?

Remember Satan's Objective!

But Satan wants to destroy the Jewish people. He doesn't want God's promises concerning us to be fulfilled, and he wants us to call God a liar.

Over the centuries Satan has found many willing to do his will; and as a result, many attempts have been made to bring about Jewish genocide. But even the most satanically energized people have been unable to destroy God's people. In fact, Napoleon Bonaparte is quoted as saying, "Bring me a Jewish person, and I will show you why I believe in God."

I cannot explain why Satan has always found people eager to do his bidding—to try to exterminate the Jewish people—but he has. And he has continually used different strategies to deceive them and make them serve him. Often it is fear. Sometimes it is jealousy. In Egypt it was fear that the Jews would grow in numbers and strength and join themselves to Egypt's enemies. In Babylon it was that the Jews worshiped only one God and would not bow down to their gods. In Russia, in the early decades of this century, it was the accusation that the Jews were Christ-killers that inflamed the Cossacks and other groups to launch pogroms against them.

And what ploy did Satan use with Hitler? The ploy of the superior race versus the inferior race. Only fair-skinned, fair-haired, blue-eyed Aryans, Hitler believed, were entitled to freedom and prosperity and the privileges of the world. Germany had to be rid of all others. They were subhuman, inferior, the cause of her problems.

So Hitler—like Haman, the villain in the biblical book of Esther—took it upon himself to purge Germany and then the entire world of the Jews, the mortal enemy.

There Were Wonderful People Who Opposed Hitler

Many Christians cried out in outrage as the news of what was happening in Germany became known. A special memorial was created in Israel to honor Oskar Schindler for his role in saving more than a thousand Jewish people from certain death. And outside of Y'ad Vashem in Jerusalem stand rows of stately trees, each one marked with a plaque listing the name of one of the "righteous Gentiles" who helped Jewish people during the Holocaust. One of these trees is dedicated to the memory of the wonderful Corrie ten Boom, who with her family hid Jews in her home.

Many Gentiles, Christian and non-Christian alike, called out to the leaders of the world to stop Hitler. But not enough.

Something happened to the conscience of the Church during those years. Something also happened to the conscience of the world. We will never know what really happened, but among the possible explanations: Satan found a larger and larger group of people to buy into the idea that because the Jewish people rejected Jesus as their Messiah, they deserved to be exterminated.

Where Was God?

Let's turn now to that big question, Where was God during the Holocaust? We must begin with what we know of God in the Bible. He is the Creator of all things. He is both all-wise and all-powerful. He could have prevented the Holocaust. In Scripture He is portrayed as the loving God who regards Israel as "the apple of his eye" (Deuteronomy 32:10; Zechariah 2:8).

Where was He, then, when His beloved people were being destroyed?

The only answer we can give to those who charge God with being helpless, remote and unmoved throughout the Hitler era is that He was with His people in their suffering in much the same way as He was 3,400 years ago when His people were oppressed generation after generation in Egypt:

> The Lord said, "I have indeed seen the misery of my people in Egypt. I have heard them crying out because of their slave drivers, and I am concerned about their suffering."
>
> Exodus 3:7

90

We must believe God is always in the midst of His people, bearing with their sorrow, their sufferings and their longing for deliverance. But we must also believe that God's ordering of the circumstances surrounding the Jewish people is always subject to His larger purposes for them. I for one cannot get away from the certainty that God was at Auschwitz, Belsen and all the other death camps—indeed, wherever His Jewish people were undergoing unspeakable suffering. This causes me to think of the pain of God. I cannot accept the concept of an impersonal, helpless God, remote from His people and indifferent to their anguish.

I am also conscious of God's ultimate purposes. Within a few years of Satan's most successful attempt to obliterate the Jewish people, the State of Israel came into being by decree of the United Nations. What prompted such a decree? Nothing less than a horrible sense of guilt. It was the victorious Allies, after all, who had failed to do anything for the Jewish people during the long Hitlerite oppression. Since the Arab nations in the Middle East were largely pro-Nazi, the United Nations felt free to redeem itself in the eyes of the Jews whom they had failed so badly. If there had been no Holocaust, there would not have been a State of Israel.

Does this mean that God's worldwide redemptive plan necessitated Israel's return to her land, which God made possible through the suffering of His people in the Holocaust? Is He not in control of history?

Application

Now we come to the application I want you to take with you from this chapter. I have shared my memories and understanding of some of the events surrounding World

War II, trusting that when the pieces of the puzzle are put together, you will see the big picture. I want to help you see and remember that big picture.

Each of us must realize that, as individuals, we do not have to participate in actions contrary to the will of God in order to sin. Many times we can sin by doing nothing (see James 4:17). And the fact is, in the face of Hitler's anti-Semitism and determination to make war against Germany's neighbors, millions of Christians did nothing.

We who are followers of Messiah Jesus must never again sit by silently while another Hitler tries to do the will of Satan. Remember, Satan is a liar and the father of lies, and he is still at work trying to discredit God. He still has his willing servants in the Mideast. He has other willing servants in Argentina. He has raised up new ones in Germany and in the former Soviet Union. Most recently he has been trying his hand in the United States, and he is having some success.

This is why we must not be unmindful of Satan's ways and that he still seeks "to steal and kill and destroy" (John 10:10). He still wants to destroy the Jewish people in order to make God out to be a liar.

We must remember the promises of God to His people and the relationship He wants His Church to have with them. Jesus wants us to love them, because He loves them. He wants us to care for them, because He cares for them. He wants us to pray for them, because He prays for them.

But consider this: You will not love the Jewish people and care for them and pray for them effectively until you come to know and understand them. This is what I trust will happen as you read the next four chapters.

PART

Increasing Your Understanding

Who is a Jew? What does it mean to be a Jew? What do today's Jews believe about God and the Bible? What do they think about Jesus? We will explore all these questions and more in the four chapters of this section.

Who Is a Jew?

When I was a kid, the question "Who is a Jew?" would have seemed very strange. Almost all the guys in my crowd were first-generation American Jews. My parents, as I have said, were from Russia, while the parents of some of my friends came from Poland and Romania and Latvia. They came to America to escape the pogroms and persecution they experienced in Europe, and to make good lives for themselves and their kids. Most spoke with heavy Yiddish accents. Many never did become fluent in English. They were simply Jews, as anyone could tell by looking at them or listening to them.

But I don't want you to have a caricature in your mind when you think of the Jewish people. In Part 1 of this book, we took a brief trip through history and saw how misperceptions of the Jewish people actually had roots in the theology of the Church Fathers. In this section I want to build on the foundation we have laid and help you gain insight about who the Jewish people really are.

Let's begin by remembering that not all Jews in the early twentieth century were immigrants. Many had come decades earlier. They no longer spoke with foreign accents. They were no longer concerned primarily with survival. Many were highly educated and had become doctors and lawyers and judges and accountants and leaders in every kind of business. They no longer lived in tenements on the Lower East Side of New York. Some lived on Park Avenue. Some lived in Beverly Hills.

Consider this astonishing fact from postwar Europe, cited by Dagobert D. Runes in *The Hebrew Impact on Western Culture* (Philosophical Library of New York, 1951):

> Half the German Nobel prizewinners were men of Jewish descent. Six hundred thousand Jews of pre-war Germany produced as many Nobel prizewinners as sixty million Germans, Herrenfolk that showed its gratitude to the men who so tremendously helped in their growth by massacring the Jewish people of Europe.

p. ix

Here's another eye-opening fact, cited by David L. Larsen in *Jews, Gentiles and the Church* (Discovery House, 1995): While making up less than one-half of one percent of the world's population, Jews have received twelve percent of all Nobel prizes awarded.

Leonard C. Yaseen, an evangelical Christian, has done an excellent job listing the contributions of Jewish men and women to our society. In his book *The Jesus Connection* (Crossroad, 1985), Yaseen lists hundreds of outstanding Jewish people. Of these I will list only 54, many of whose names you will recognize. As you read them, try to visualize their faces. You will recognize tremendous differences among them, yet they are all Jews.

In the field of science:

Albert Einstein	*Sigmund Freud*	*Arthur Kornberg*
Edwin Land	*Jonas Salk*	*David Sarnoff*
Charles Steinmetz	*Gerald Swope*	*Selman Waksman*

In the field of public service:

Bernard Baruch	*Louis D. Brandeis*	*Arthur Burns*
Benjamin N. Cardoza	*Felix Frankfurter*	*Ernest Gruening*
Jacob Javits	*Henry Kissinger*	*Herbert Lehman*

In the field of entertainment:

Woody Allen	*Stephen Spielberg*	*Barbra Streisand*
Ed Asner	*Jack Benny*	*Milton Berle*
George Burns	*Sid Caesar*	*Tony Curtis*
Goldie Hawn	*Dustin Hoffman*	*Mike Nichols*
Michael Landon	*Paul Newman*	*William Shatner*
Leonard Nimoy	*Tony Randall*	*Mike Wallace*

In the field of music:

Irving Berlin	*Leonard Bernstein*	*Victor Borge*
Arthur Fiedler	*George Gershwin*	*Oscar Hammerstein*
Vladimir Horowitz	*Jerome Kern*	*Itzhak Perlman*

In the fields of journalism, theatre and literature:

Ted Koppel	*Joseph Heller*	*Lillian Hellman*
Ann Landers	*Arthur Miller*	*Edwin Newman*
Dorothy Parker	*Joseph Pulitzer*	*Theodore S. White*

I do not mean to say that the 54 people on this list have the greatest talent America has ever known. And I am sure you know the names of many Jewish people not listed—jurists and statesmen and scientists and comedians and actors and singers and painters and dancers. But this list does suggest the contribution Jewish people have made to our nation and to the world—a disproportionate contribution when you consider that Jewish people make up less than three percent of America's population. No caricatures here, do you agree?

What is it that makes these people Jews? Indeed, what or who is the final authority on that subject?

Who Gets to Decide?

The question "Who is a Jew?" is enormously significant to Jewish people today. Is being Jewish a matter of birth or religion or culture or choice? And just who gets to make that decision?

The Nazis

In Hitler's day the Nazis decided. Anyone with a drop of Jewish blood was called a Jew and, they declared, deserved extermination.

So Jesus would have faced the gas chamber. All of the apostles would have followed, even Luke (although he was probably not Jewish), because of his identification with the Jewish people.

The Synagogue

Today the synagogue often determines Jewish identity. A Jewish friend of mine, a successful attorney, fell in love with a woman who was not Jewish and married her while he was still in law school. Over the years they had two wonderful children.

His wife—let's call her Joan—never converted to Judaism. Even so, in order to provide their children with a Jewish upbringing, she became a member of a Conservative synagogue. Joan became more Jewish than Larry, who often worked late on Friday nights and on Saturdays and rarely attended the synagogue. Joan was the one who took the children to religious school and to services each week. She joined the sisterhood of the synagogue. Because her last name was Jewish and she was so involved, most people thought she was Jewish.

Then their son approached the age of twelve, time for a boy to enroll for training to become, at thirteen, a *bar mitzvah* (son of the commandment). That was when the bomb dropped. Because Joan was not Jewish and had not converted to Judaism, the synagogue did not regard her children as Jewish, and her son could not be bar mitzvahed.

Joan and her son were devastated, but Larry was furious. How could this be?

When the rabbi saw the extent of the family's pain, he offered a solution: If their son would convert to Judaism, he could have his bar mitzvah.

After agonizing over this offer for days, Joan and Larry decided that their son should accept the rabbi's recommendation and convert so he could go on with his bar mitzvah. But I am sure it was a bittersweet event for them.

The point of the story: To the Jewish people, Jewish identity is crucial.

The State of Israel

The State of Israel has been wrestling with the Jewish identity question for decades. Let's try to understand why.

A man born to two Jewish parents has nothing to do with the Jewish religion or culture anymore and does not identify himself as a Jew. Is he a Jew?

A woman has one Jewish grandparent, but no one else in her family is Jewish. Is she Jewish?

A man comes from a mixed marriage—one parent Jewish, the other not. Is he a Jew?

In 1950, just two years after Israel became a State, the Law of Return was enacted. Its primary purpose was to make certain a Jewish majority would dwell in the land. The Law of Return permitted people with only one Jewish grandparent to become citizens of the State of Israel. This law was well received and millions of Jews became citizens of Israel without difficulty.

In 1958, however, the religious parties precipitated a Cabinet crisis because they wanted the government to define the word *Jew* as the Orthodox rabbis defined it. (See Appendix 2 on p. 260 for an explanation of the different denominations in American Judaism—the general term that covers all the diverse forms of Jewish religion.) This issue created a government crisis, so the officials sought guidance from Jewish communities outside Israel. Ultimately they decided that even if a Jewish person forsakes the Jewish religion, that person is still a Jew so long as he or she does not accept another religion.

What religion did they have in mind? Not Zen Buddhism. Not Hare Krishna. Not humanism. No, the only religion they objected to was Christianity.

Commenting on messianic Jews—Jews who believe Jesus is the Messiah—in an article in *Washington Jewish Week* (May 23, 1996), Rabbi A. James Rudin, director of interreligious affairs for the American Jewish Committee, said, "They're not Jews, clearly." And Jerome Epstein, executive vice president of United Synagogue, in the same article: "My own personal conclusion is that for purposes of this question, a messianic Jew is not a Jew."

Arthur W. Kac in his book *The Messiahship of Jesus* (Baker Book House, 1986) explains:

> The Supreme Court [of Israel], strictly speaking, acted on behalf of the State of Israel, but in reality it spoke for all Jews. Under the influence of Rabbinic Judaism the word Jew has, among other things, come to mean opposition to Jesus Christ. Actually, since the first century much of Judaism developed as a reaction against Christianity.
>
> pp. 139–140

Two other quotes in Kac's book illustrate the importance to Jewish people of the question of identity.

> It is the rejection of Jesus as Christ that binds American Jews together. It is by the rejection of the Messiahship of Jesus that we proclaim to the world that we are still Jews.
>
> p. 140

And also:

> If a Jew accepts a [Jewish convert to Christianity] as good a Jew as himself, then he automatically goes halfway along the road to Christianity. He endangers the entire *raison d'être* of the existence of the Jewish people.
>
> p. 140

We may shake our heads in dismay over these statements, yet we can readily understand why they were made. Self-preservation is a powerful force!

101

The Rabbis

The rabbis want to be the final decision-makers on the question "Who is a Jew?" But even among rabbis there is disagreement. Orthodox rabbis insist that unless your mother is Jewish, you are not Jewish. Most Conservative rabbis agree. But most Reform rabbis enlarge the definition and say that if either of your parents is Jewish, you are Jewish.

What if you were not born to Jewish parents but converted to Judaism? Are you Jewish?

Sammy Davis, Jr., converted to Judaism. Did that make him a Jew? Most Jews would say, "Not really." Converts to Judaism become not Jews but proselytes to Judaism. (Their children, however, are considered Jews.)

But there is a wrinkle in this, too. The Orthodox community in Israel does not recognize conversion to Judaism unless that conversion is overseen in the prescribed manner by an Orthodox rabbi. And if you are converted in a Conservative or Reform ceremony, your conversion is not accepted.

The Final Authority

Who, then, is the final authority? To whom do we look for the answer to the question "Who is a Jew?" To the synagogue? To the State of Israel? To the Orthodox or Conservative or Reform or Reconstructionist or Humanistic rabbis of the world? To the Jewish community itself?

Should we not be looking to God for our answer?

The first time the term *Jews* appears in Scripture is the King James translation of 2 Kings 16:6 (the NIV translates it *men of Judah*). The word *Jew* comes from *Judah*, the name of the fourth son of Jacob. To understand the origin of this term, we must refer to the covenant God cut with a specific people. How did God define who they would be? The Bible does not say all the descendants of Abraham would be in a covenant relationship with Him. If it did, there would be no covenantal difference between Arabs and Jews. Nor does it say that all the descendants of Abraham and Isaac are God's covenant people. No, the Bible refers continually to *the descendants of Abraham, Isaac and Jacob* as God's covenant people, the apple of His eye.

We must also remember that Jacob's name was changed to Israel (Genesis 32:28). For a very long time afterward we were known as the children of Israel. Politically the word *Jew* referred to the tribe that bore Judah's name. Geographically it referred to the Southern Kingdom in the Promised Land. Practically speaking it now refers to all the physical descendants of Abraham, Isaac and Jacob, wherever they are in the world.

Most children are taught that there are five races in the world: white, brown, red, yellow and black. Yet I have often heard people talk about the Jewish "race." We are not a race. Some Jews are white. Some Jews are brown. Some Jews are yellow. Some Jews are black. Some Jews may even be red.

Throughout both the older and newer Covenants, the descendants of Abraham, Isaac and Jacob are referred to as a distinct *nation*, a distinct *people*. Here are just three references to consider.

In Genesis 12:2 God said to Abram, "I will make you into a great nation." God repeated His promise in Genesis 35:11: "A nation and a community of nations will come from you, and kings will come from your body." And in Luke 23:2, when the Pharisees sought to condemn Jesus, we read that "they began to accuse him, saying, 'We have found this man subverting our nation. He opposes payment of taxes to Caesar and claims to be Christ, a king.'"

So from an ethnic point of view, we can say that even if a person born of Jewish parents is now an atheist, he or she is still a Jew. A person born of a Jewish mother who is now a Hare Krishna is still a Jew. A person whose mother is Jewish but who is now into Zen Buddhism is still a Jew. A person whose mother is Jewish and who now follows the religion of humanism is still a Jew.

What shall we say, then, about the person whose mother is Jewish and who now believes in Jesus?

Why Did God Choose the Jewish People?

We become Jews by birth. Biblically the line is determined by the father. Rabbinically the line is determined by the mother. But the ethnic determination of a person's Jewishness is not the highest authority. There is a much higher authority making the decision.

In Genesis 17 God said to Abram:

> "I will establish my covenant as an everlasting covenant between me and you and your descendants after you for the generations to come, to be your God and the God of your descendants after you."

verse 7

The decision to choose the Jews, separating them from all the nations of the world, was made by almighty God for His own reasons. Accordingly it seems incongruous that any of us would try to establish our identities apart from God. Deuteronomy 14:2 states it this way: "Out of all the peoples on the face of the earth, the LORD has chosen you to be his treasured possession."

Why did God choose us? Deuteronomy 7 advises us:

> The LORD did not set his affection on you and choose you because you were more numerous than other peoples, for you were the fewest of all peoples. But it was because

the LORD loved you and kept the oath he swore to your forefathers that he brought you out with a mighty hand and redeemed you from the land of slavery, from the power of Pharaoh king of Egypt.

verses 7–8

What did God have in mind? Jeremiah 24:7 offers a clue: "I will give them a heart to know me, that I am the LORD. They will be my people, and I will be their God, for they will return to me with all their heart."

And in Isaiah 43:21 God refers to "the people I formed for myself that they may proclaim my praise."

There is no getting away from the fact that God chose us, the weakest and least numerous of all nations on earth, so that He could reveal His greatness through us. And He gave us an assignment: We are to proclaim His praise to all people.

What Was It about Abraham?

With this thought firmly established, let's raise another question: Why did God choose to enter a covenantal relationship with Abraham? Of all people on earth, why did God choose Abraham? Was Abraham so special? Or was it that God would make him special?

Genesis provides two answers. First, in Genesis 12:2 God said: "I will make you into a great nation and I will bless you; I will make your name great, and you will be a blessing." Clearly that is what happened. God did what He said He would do. Through Abraham and the chosen people, God has blessed the whole world with the coming of the Messiah. Further, He made it possible for us to be a blessing in every land to which we have been driven.

105

Genesis 18 declares a second reason for God's choice of Abraham:

> Then the LORD said, "Shall I hide from Abraham what I am about to do? Abraham will surely become a great and powerful nation, and all nations on earth will be blessed through him. For I have chosen him, so that he will direct his children and his household after him to keep the way of the LORD. . . ."

> verses 17–19

The spiritual aspect of God's choice must not be missed. God chose Abraham for a purpose: He would entrust His truth to him. Abraham, in turn, would be faithful not only in his personal response to that truth, but as its faithful custodian—guarding the truth, teaching it to his children, instilling in them the determination to pass it on to their children after them, so that they, too, would keep the way of the Lord.

We must never lose sight of the fact that it is God who has determined what we have been chosen for. Indeed, to consider ourselves Jewish without reference to God's covenantal relationship with us and His purpose for us is both ironic and tragic. It is He who chose us from among all nations. It is He who defined us as a people. It is He who has preserved us. It is He who gave us our Mosaic covenant. It is He who gave us our New Covenant. It is He who has declared our mission to be "a light for the Gentiles, that you may bring my salvation to the ends of the earth" (Isaiah 49:6).

Our ethnicity as descendants of Abraham, Isaac and Jacob is important, but not to be worshiped! We must never lose sight of the One who chose us. He alone is to be worshiped. Further, we must never lose sight of His purpose in choosing us: We are to declare His greatness to the uttermost parts of the earth. Again I remind you that the word *Jew* comes from the name *Judah,* whose name means "praise." In God's sight we Jews have been called to be praisers of God—the one God, the God of Abraham, Isaac and Jacob. We are to serve Him, to teach our children to keep His ways, to represent Him to the nations.

Accordingly, I put before you a thesis you may never have thought about: Jews who are atheists or agnostics or humanists or Zen Buddhists or Hare Krishna or any other religion, even Jews who seldom think about God, can hardly be considered praisers of God. So in a biblical sense, they can hardly be considered Jews. I am saying that any attempt to assign us an identity apart from God's Word is only self-serving.

Some say that what unites Jewish people today, despite all our diversity, is our determination to agree that Jesus is not the Messiah. We will discuss this later, but suffice it for now to say that this is obviously not true. God knows who His covenant people are, the thousands who make up His believing remnant (see Romans 11:5).

With this background established, we are now ready to consider a related and vital question: What does it mean to be a Jew today?

7

What Does It Mean to Be a Jew Today?

Does this question surprise you? After spending so much time in the last chapter exploring the question "Who is a Jew?", does it seem strange for me to ask, "What does it mean to be a Jew today?" And besides, won't different people supply different answers to that question?

Of course they will. But the emphasis in my question is on the word *today*. Being Jewish meant one thing in Jesus' day. It meant another thing during the Crusades, yet another to those who lived in a Polish ghetto at the turn of the century. But how about today? What does being Jewish mean at the dawn of the twenty-first century?

I want you not just to read but to experience the contents of this chapter, so you will understand why there is no one way to relate to, or communicate with, Jewish people.

109

How We See Ourselves

In the last chapter we reviewed the names of many well-known people. Some of them were or are Orthodox Jews. Others might be members of Conservative or Reform congregations. Some might be atheists. I suspect, however, that most of those still living are non-observant, secular Jews.

We saw in the last chapter that being Jewish is a matter of birth. But the *meaning* of being Jewish is another matter.

I love being a Jew. I am awed by our history. I grieve over our persecution and am amazed how we have survived. I love our people. I delight in our culture. I love our music. I am joyous in our dance. I devour our foods. I delight in our achievements. I am proud because of what we have given the world. And, yes, I even speak Yiddish.

I have been to Israel thirteen times and rejoice in what she has accomplished. I understand the conflicts Israel faces today. I understand her longing for peace. I understand many of the divisions among her political parties. I fear for what might befall her, surrounded as she is by hostile peoples.

How different am I from other Jews in America? From other Jews in Israel or Europe or South America? Is our identity based on our support for Israel? Is it based on our synagogue affiliation?

While a very small percentage of our people are Orthodox in their beliefs, most Jews in Israel and in Jewish communities all over the world are secular. We may belong to a synagogue, but most of us aren't really sure we believe in God. We go to the synagogue when there is a special occasion or for the high holidays of Rosh Hashanah and Yom Kippur. But aside from religious school for our kids, the synagogue plays only a minor role in most of our lives.

So is our identity based on our religious affiliation?

As I thought about the need for this chapter, I began to ask people I knew or met in my travels what being Jewish meant to them. I wasn't surprised by their answers. Many spoke of our heritage. Indeed, our Jewish heritage is awesome. Think about it. My family line—without dilution or interruption, to the best of my knowledge—traces all the way back to Abraham!

That's true for most of the Jewish people I know. We are talking here about four thousand years of history, of taking the worst the world has to offer and surviving. Our heritage includes some of the greatest thinkers and philosophers of all time. And what about our artists and musicians and dancers and writers? This is a heritage of which any people can be proud! And who doesn't smile and clap his hands at the sound of *klezmer* music, the Jewish music of Eastern Europe, or the Israeli folk music of today? Our music can be so joyous that it makes us jump up and dance. It can also make us weep.

Some joke as they speak about the uniqueness of Jewish food. Is there anything better in this world than a good corned beef sandwich? And where would we be without sour pickles? And Mama's brisket? And chopped liver? And gefilte fish? And heartburn?

My wife insists there is no such thing as Jewish food. She argues that because Jews have lived all over the world, they have incorporated endless variations into their diet, creatively improving on the originals in the process. That may be true, but if my cabbage soup isn't made with raisins, I question whether it is really Jewish cabbage soup!

Some insist that being Jewish automatically endows one with a special sense of humor. In many ways that is true. Over the thousands of years of our existence we have suf-

111

fered enormously, yet we have laughed. We have laughed at the hopelessness of our situation. We have laughed at those who persecuted us. We have even laughed at ourselves and our customs. We laugh because it is easier to laugh than to cry. And haven't we given some wonderful comedians to the world?

Others speak about our culture and ethics. Yes, we can be proud of them, too. It is unfortunately true that among the unscrupulous people of the world, we find Jewish people, but a sense of fairness and rightness and responsibility for our own behavior is deeply imbedded in most of us. Much of our concern for ethics comes from the Word of God and the commentaries in our Talmud that tell us how we are to live with one another. Much of our lifestyle, and particularly our ways of coping with hostility, come from our life experience in the ghettos of the world. We had to be fair with one another and take care of one another, for there was no one else to take care of us. We were *mishpocha*. We were family.

And didn't we give the world its understanding of the one God? Hallowed be His holy name.

Some "Average Jews" Respond

For 338 pages in his book *Heritage: Civilization and the Jews* (Summit, 1984), Abba Eban, Israel's former foreign minister, ambassador to the United States and to the United Nations, describes the splendor of his Jewish heritage. As he concludes his overview, Eban makes this statement:

> . . . the Jewish future is uncharted; there are no certainties ahead. But a people that takes its past into its future with such intensity of recollection, such poignancy of affliction, and such creative vitality will not easily renounce

112

its hope of planting its seed in future civilizations and taking its share of the common harvest from their midst. And so, after thousands of years, the Jews stand as they have so often stood, small, dispersed, vulnerable, but still inspired by a large and spacious ambition, still hoping to see great visions and to dream great dreams, the people with a voice whose echoes never die.

p. 338

An impressive statement from a man who has spent most of his life studying and being deeply involved in Jewish and Israeli life! But it doesn't speak of what being Jewish means to the average Jewish person walking the streets of Milwaukee or Liverpool or Paris or Toronto or Sydney.

I directed this question to more than one hundred people in the United States, all in their mid-thirties or early forties. You can be sure I received some interesting responses! Here are excerpts from just a few.

Jill said:

Being Jewish is an identity I inherited from both of my parents. It means celebrating the holidays of Passover, Rosh Hashanah, Yom Kippur and Chanukah. As long as I accompany my parents to the temple with my sisters, I fulfill all that my parents require of me as a Jew.

Michael responded:

For a long time I was embarrassed by my Jewishness and didn't want others to know I was Jewish. I was one of only two Jewish kids in my public school.

Ed said:

When I was a young child, the God of Israel was very real to me. When I recited our ancient declaration, "Hear, O Is-

113

rael, the Lord our God is one; blessed be His glorious name forever and ever" in Hebrew each night before going to sleep [the watchword of the Jewish faith, taken from Deuteronomy 6:4], I would sense His presence. I thought this awesome and fearful Person would get me if I didn't obey the Ten Commandments, especially the one that says, "Honor your father and mother." As I grew up, I became more sophisticated and worldly wise. I lost this fear of God and became more concerned with the acceptance of my peer group. Since none of them, Jews or Gentiles, believed in God, and since I see no evidence of His presence in the Jewish community, I have concluded that God is just a convenient sociological myth. In many ways my being Jewish is painful, scary, boring and empty.

A different Jill made these points:

Being a daughter of a survivor of the Holocaust and of Russian Jewish immigrants, I feel that being Jewish is a burden. "Remember and never forget the affliction of your ancestors," I was taught. I remember feeling a lot of weight and very little joy from these memories. I understand little of what goes on in our synagogue because I don't understand Hebrew. To me, then, being Jewish means good food, music that touches my heart, and stressful family gatherings. Even though there are many difficult aspects of being Jewish, I feel special and strong because of them.

Alberta shared this:

For me, being Jewish means family holiday get-togethers, lighting candles on Friday nights and going to the synagogue. Being Jewish also means pain.

Jeff commented:

My father was very active in the Jewish community, and that gave us a measure of prestige. We had Shabbat dinner at our home every Friday night and I went to the synagogue three times a year. I've always believed that part of being Jewish is being sad or unhappy. That's all being Jewish means to me.

Steve said:

Being Jewish means having an identity, belonging to a people who are special to God, an identity with Zionism and the land of Israel. I take pride in being part of my "special" people.

Rachel echoed Steve's sentiment:

Being Jewish is part of my identity. It is who I am.

Carol responded this way:

For me, being Jewish is a cultural thing. I was not formally trained in Judaism, but my mom taught me some of our Hebrew prayers. Mostly being Jewish means special foods, a somewhat different sense of humor and being liberal and intellectual.

Cheryl offered:

For me being Jewish is defined by what I do and do not do, what I believe and do not believe. Beyond that, being Jewish endows me with a certain pride in being part of a people who, even though they were a persecuted minority, have always made a great impact on the world throughout our history.

Peter said:

Being Jewish means having an identity with a people, a heritage. God doesn't seem to be at the center of who we are. Instead we seem to honor ourselves and our achievements in the face of great opposition. Being Jewish means honoring the customs and traditions of our fathers, which bind us together as a people.

Victoria, a recent immigrant from the Ukraine, said:

My only real identity as a Jew is that we are a hated and persecuted people, though special to God.

An anonymous responder said this:

Since I was born in Israel, my nationality has always been extremely important to me. My being Jewish is a fact of life.

Another Jeff said this:

Judaism has been empty and uncertain for me. I identify with Israel and the Jewish nation, but nothing else much matters. I really am not concerned about much else.

Richard said:

Being Jewish, to me, has an extremely traditional meaning. And there is pride. Of course, I suppose that being Jewish is an intellectual experience exercised from my head and not at all from my heart. Though my family celebrates the Jewish feasts, I do not.

And from Chuck:

Being Jewish to me means celebrating the holidays and going to services occasionally.

Finally, from Barbara:

Being Jewish is my historical and cultural identity. I was not raised in any religious context. We are secular, intellectual Jews. For us, being Jewish doesn't involve anything religious. Being Jewish means we value education and being intellectual. It means political and social involvement in our community. It also means fearing anti-Semitism, since my mother was in a concentration camp.

Although I did not have the opportunity to do so, I suppose that if I went into an extremely Orthodox section of New York City and asked the same question—"What does being Jewish mean to you?"—I would get significantly different answers. They would probably have to do with the study of Talmud and keeping a kosher home and observing the Sabbath. Even there, however, I suspect that cultural and historical identity would be among the chief explanations of what it means to be a Jew today.

Cultural Characteristics

Most Jewish people today are involved only superficially with the religious practices of Judaism. Most are humanists. Some are agnostics. Others are atheists.

Those of us who want to go to a traditional synagogue or to a Reform temple (see Appendix 2 for a discussion of the different denominations in Jewish life today) have a whole range of services to choose from. There are Orthodox, Conservative, Reform, Reconstructionist, even gay and lesbian synagogues. Each has its own point of view. Clearly Jewish people today throughout the world hold a wide range of beliefs and unbeliefs.

Some of us rarely go to synagogue. Some go fairly regularly. Some don't go at all.

Significantly, there is no one person in the Jewish community who can speak clearly and powerfully to us, any

117

more than there is any one person who can speak clearly and powerfully *for* us.

We are deeply involved, however, in taking care of our own. Many consider Jewish philanthropy to be the eighth wonder of the world. We care for our elderly. We care for our young. We have Jewish community centers and Jewish hospitals and Jewish day schools and Jewish universities and Jewish sanitariums. We have the United Jewish Appeal and the United Jewish Federation. We have Jewish poor houses and Jewish country clubs. We have Jewish newspapers. And we still have Jewish matchmakers.

Back in the second chapter of this book, I mentioned *Fiddler on the Roof*, not only because it would help you understand where my parents came from, but because this play and film helped to open the hearts of people all around the world to some of what has happened to us as a people and how we have emerged despite it. The film *Schindler's List*, which shows how one German businessman saved Jews during the Holocaust, has also had a positive impact. It dramatized for a worldwide audience some of the horrors six million people had to go through simply because they were Jews.

As long as we are listing some of the characteristics of Jewish culture, let's not forget the effect of the *intifada* (Palestinian uprising) and Middle East terrorism, even though at first some of the incidents were staged.

On one tour of Israel, I paused with the group for refreshments in the shade beneath the bridge leading to the Damascus Gate in Jerusalem. It was very hot that June day, and we were drinking Cokes and enjoying the break. Suddenly we heard clamor and shouting. Our guide told us to stay where we were while she went up to investigate. A few moments later she returned, shaking her head and smiling. A TV crew, she reported, had set up their cameras. On cue a demonstration broke out. Moments later, when the scene had been captured on videotape, the demonstration ended.

Later came the battle of the daily TV videobites, which showed Palestinian teenagers throwing rocks at Israeli troops. Obviously this footage was intended to promote the cause of the Palestinians, a people to whom much wrong has been done. Still, one could not help seeing the frustration of the Israeli soldiers who were being pelted with stones day after day and required to exercise restraint.

Then, after Gaza became a Palestinian city and the Israeli soldiers left, the terrible suicide bombings started. Since Israel's first accord with the Palestinians, according to Israeli Zion Anati, quoted in a front-page article in *The Washington Post* on May 26, 1996, "we've had over 200 dead." In 1995 and 1996 alone, several dozen innocent Jewish men, women and children were blown apart as they rode their buses in Jerusalem and Tel Aviv, while Hamas, a radical Islamic group that claimed responsibility for these bombings, rejoiced.

Put yourself in Israeli shoes for a moment. How would you react if the bombings took place in your neighborhood? What if your own mother or father or husband or wife or sister or brother or son or daughter were killed on one of those buses? What would you tell your children? How eager would you be to get to work if you had to take that same bus tomorrow?

The crisis of having to deal with terrorism, sometimes on a daily basis, has helped the world to see what we Jews have to put up with in our search for acceptance and peace.

A Flashback

When my daughter Judy was finishing religious school and preparing for her confirmation in our Reform congregation, we obtained the book *Challenge to Confirmands* by Arnold Jacob Wolf (Scribe Publications, 1963). Just recently I picked up that book to remind myself of the challenge:

> To be a Jew is to be free. One of Judaism's best advertised advantages is freedom, the right to think things out in our own way for ourselves. We Jews do not feel bound to accept or believe anything very specific. Our consciences are absolutely our own. Jews are divided into many schools of thought. Even within liberal Judaism itself there are many different beliefs, some directly contradicting others. Yet people who disagree belong to the same congregation, pray from the same prayer book, learn from the same rabbi. Though we differ, we can be very important to each other. And this, too, is a mark of our freedom.

This statement puts our opening question into focus. The answer to the question "What does it mean to be a Jew today?" really does depend on whom you ask.

As I said earlier, I wanted you not just to read but to experience the contents of this chapter, so you would know there is no one way to relate to, or communicate with, the Jewish people to whom you will be reaching out. I hope this chapter has given you more insight than you had before.

And now, to increase your understanding even more, it is time to raise a more specific question.

8

What Do Today's Jews Believe about God and the Bible?

In the last chapter we probed the meaning of being Jewish. The people whose comments I quoted in my informal survey said little (as you probably noticed) about how they felt about God and the Bible. But because that subject is critical to understanding Jewish people today, it is appropriate for us to consider it now.

My wife Ethel and I enjoy reading Jewish newspapers. Most of the papers distributed in the U.S. are written in English, primarily by Jews, for Jews and about Jewish themes and concerns. They contain commercial advertising as well as advertising from synagogues, Jewish groups and individuals.

Some time ago, just before the Jewish New Year and Day of Atonement, I was reading several synagogue ads to see how they would describe their congregations. Some of these ads intrigued me.

One synagogue referred to itself as "not believing in the supernatural."

"Not believing in the supernatural?" I repeated aloud. "They are saying they don't believe in God!"

Then I saw an ad for a gay and lesbian synagogue, and another ad that read, "Finding the exotic and the spiritual in our own backyard." One ad in the matchmaker section read, "I express my Judaism through nature and Reconstructionist values." Another ad touted "The Society for Humanistic Judaism."

Why do I start this chapter with this information? To remind you once again how divergent a people we Jews are, and how far many of us have come from our biblical mandate to bring the nations of the earth to God. In many ways we have embraced a Judaism without God.

Do you know what the main preoccupations of Jewish people are? Let me list a few. The worship of being Jewish. The preservation of our people and the State of Israel. The significance of Jewish culture. The promotion of Jewish issues. Keeping a kosher home. Going to the synagogue on Rosh Hashanah and Yom Kippur. Celebrating Passover with our families. Being liberal and intellectual. Giving our kids "a good Jewish education." Being successful. Taking care of our young and elderly. Our need for Jewish community.

No one would disagree that most of these represent noble causes. But where is God in our lives?

Who Is Your God?

I mentioned back in the opening chapter that on July 2, 1975, the day before I confessed Jesus as Lord of my life, a very special lady asked me some pointed questions: "Who is your God? Is He the God of our fathers—the God of Abraham, Isaac and Jacob? Or are you worshiping false gods like your business, your home, your wife, your children? What do you spend your time thinking about? Whom do you worship?"

The vast majority of the approximately eighteen million Jewish people scattered throughout the world today would have to stop and think before attempting to answer these questions honestly. No one can speak for all of us (as I have already pointed out) and no one can speak *to* all of us. But we all have to face the same questions: Who is our God? How do we think about Him? What do we believe about Him? Do we believe our Bible is His Word to us, or is it just a fable or the story of the Jewish people? Is God relevant in our lives?

Many say He is not. Others hope God exists, but are not at all sure that He does. Still others want God to exist in the hope that He will protect us, provide for us and preserve us as a people; but they are not sure that such longings are not based on a myth.

The majority of Jewish people, I suspect, are afraid to say God does not exist, even though they are not absolutely sure that He does. To play it safe, most of us Jews go to a synagogue from time to time, especially on the high holidays, thinking, *If God is up there, maybe this will satisfy Him. If He isn't, I haven't wasted too much time.* In many ways and for many Jews, going to the synagogue has become a matter of identifying with our people rather than worshiping God.

Many of us have lost sight of God and His covenant with us. More and more of us in the United States, Israel and around the world have become outright humanists, declaring boldly that we do not believe in God. Our primary commitment as modern Jews is to our people and a few of the 613 commandments God gave us. (We readily ignore the rest.) The extent of our spiritual commitment is defined by whether or not we honor the Sabbath, keep a kosher home, observe some ancient rituals, give to Jewish charities—and make sure we don't believe in Jesus!

How We Lost Our Scriptures

Throughout time we Jewish people have been known as "people of the Book." So how did we become a people who don't know the Book?

Although a detailed study of Jewish history is beyond our purposes here, let's look briefly at the two major events that played an important role in turning Jewish people away from our Bible.

Event #1: The Destruction of the Temple

The destruction of the Temple in Jerusalem in 70 C.E. is the starting point for our quick overview. Let's consider it before we reflect on an even earlier incident in Jewish history.

When the Temple was destroyed, the biblically authorized sacrificial system came to an end. We Jewish people could no longer offer sacrifices in the only place where they would be acceptable. We could no longer follow the prescribed manner of obtaining the forgiveness of our sins through the sacrifice of animals. Furthermore, the high priest could no longer obtain forgiveness for us by the strict liturgy of the Temple. He could no longer enter the Holy Place or the Holy of Holies on the Day of Atonement.

How, then, could we Jews obtain forgiveness prompted by our desire for right standing with God? Without the Temple and the sacrifice system, how were we to live our lives as Jews?

The Development of Rabbinism

The answers the rabbis came up with over the ensuing centuries would become known as rabbinism or rabbinic Judaism—which is distinct from biblical Judaism. Jewish spiritual life would now focus on what the rabbis said rather than on what the Bible said.

This shift represented a major shift for the Jewish people. Rabbinism became the glue that held our people together all over the world. It built a spiritual wall around us and kept us from the outside influences of the world. That spiritual wall later became a physical wall as, for centuries, the world created ghettos to isolate and contain us. The horror of our ghetto existence must not be overlooked, although much good was done inside the ghettos of the world.

A little more than a hundred years ago, the ghetto walls, figuratively speaking, began to crumble, as Jews in Poland, Russia, Latvia, Lithuania, Romania and other neighboring countries were freed to work and live outside the ghetto. Many left to come to the New World.

With this significant physical change, a spiritual change also took place: The influence of rabbinism began to crumble.

Salvation through Works

Over many centuries of ghetto life, certain non-biblical practices and perspectives began to be emphasized. One of these was that Jews could achieve right standing with God through actions. The Bible is clear that our father Abraham achieved a right relationship with God through faith (see Genesis 15:6) and that a believing remnant in Israel realized that without faith it is impossible to please God (see Hebrews 11:6). But in the ghetto, increasing numbers of Jews came to see knowledge and action as more important than faith.

125

It didn't take too many years before redemption was understood as lying within the grasp of any Jew. Salvation was not a gift of God to be received through faith, but an award one could obtain by assuming responsibility as his or her brother's keeper.

Distinguishing from Christianity

Part of the rabbinic stress on salvation through works came as the rabbis drew a distinction between what the Jewish followers of Jesus believed and what rabbinic Judaism taught. The rabbis were determined to prove wrong the apostle Paul, who had written, "No one will be declared righteous in [God's] sight by observing the law" (Romans 3:20). Paul's view was amplified but not changed by the apostle James: "Someone will say, 'You have faith; I have deeds.' Show me your faith without deeds, and I will show you my faith by what I do" (James 2:18). Both apostles agreed that it is faith that saves, and then provokes us to live an obedient life out of gratitude to the God who saved us.

The rabbis, by contrast, stressed obedience to the Law of Moses. What you believed did not matter. You had to obey the Law. (But what of those who broke the Law?)

This distinction was maintained down through the centuries. *The Standard Jewish Encyclopedia* (Doubleday, 1959) says that "Judaism places the emphasis on practical religion rather than on dogma." *The Universal Jewish Encyclopedia* (Universal Jewish Encyclopedia, 1939) says, "Whereas Christianity emphasizes salvation by grace, Judaism stresses salvation through works."

Event #2: The Talmud Emerges

Now for the second event pivotal to the turning away of the Jewish people from the Tenach.

The Jewish community, under the influence of the rabbis, confined God's Word to what followers of Jesus call the Old Testament. In the synagogue this is referred to as the *Torah*—the first five books of Moses. Sometimes the word *Torah* is expanded to include all the Hebrew Scriptures, although the proper word for the entire Bible is the Hebrew word *Tenach*.

The Tenach was considered complete with the book of Malachi. That, the rabbis said, is when the voice of prophecy ceased. The differences between the Tenach and the King James Version of the Bible have to do primarily with the order and number of books in each. In content they are almost identical.

The Torah had to be taught and explained to the people. This was the primary duty of the priests (see Malachi 2:5–7). Except for the scrolls of the Bible, nothing was written down, so the teachers had to memorize, then transmit it orally. They taught their disciples not only what the Torah said, but their interpretations of the Torah as well. These interpretations became known as the oral law, which in many circles came to have as much importance in Jewish life as the written Law. Indeed in some places, more credence is given the oral law than the written Law.

First the Mishna

Remember with me that the Torah contains 613 specific commandments of God. Of these laws, 248 are negative in nature (the "thou shalt nots") and 365 are positive (the "thou shalts"). The Mishna is a series of writings that came into being in Babylon about 250 years before Jesus came to earth, writings that continued to be added to for hundreds of years. The Mishna is a detailed commentary on each and every one of the 613 commandments of God. (The word *Mishna* means "repetition.")

Let me give you three illustrations of what the Mishna contains.

1. Keeping Kosher

Twice in the book of Exodus (23:19; 34:26) and once in the book of Deuteronomy (14:21) we find the instruction "Thou shalt not seethe a kid in his mother's milk." That was it. That was the commandment. But what did it mean? What was the application of that commandment to the daily life of the Jewish people?

Novelist James A. Michener in *The Source* (Fawcett Crest, 1967) comments that as the rabbis considered this verse,

> three words stood out. Seethe was probably meant to include all kinds of cooking. Kid was meant to include all kinds of meat. And milk was intended to cover all possible variations of dairy products.
>
> p. 526

So the rabbis, after arriving at these conclusions, created a set of laws that observant Jews have followed for thousands of years. Milk products and meat products must be kept separate. Further, separate dishes, pots, pans, knives, forks, spoons and glasses are to be used for each—one complete set for meat dishes, another complete set for dairy dishes.

What about Passover? Because the home is to be rid of all leaven at Passover, the utensils used for dairy and meat dishes during the course of the year were to be put away at Passover time, and two completely different sets of utensils that had never been used with food that contained leaven were to be used. Michener observes:

> When in Babylonia other rabbis began to evolve other refinements even more difficult to observe. No one could

128

contest them, either. For what the rabbis were doing, in part consciously and in part unconsciously, was the creation of a body of law that would bind the Jews together as they went into exile to the Diaspora. Without a homeland the Jews would live within their law and become a nation mightier than those which had oppressed them. Without cities of their own they would as a cohesive unit help determine the destinies of cities they had not yet seen.

pp. 526–527

2. Honoring the Sabbath

Exodus 20:10–11 reads:

"The seventh day is a Sabbath to the LORD your God. On it you shall not do any work, neither you, nor your son or daughter, nor your manservant or maidservant, nor your animals, nor the alien within your gates. For in six days the LORD made the heavens and the earth, the sea, and all that is in them, but he rested on the seventh day. Therefore the LORD blessed the Sabbath day and made it holy."

This is the commandment in the Torah to keep Shabbat, the Sabbath. But how, asked the rabbis, are we to keep Shabbat as a holy day? Clearly it was a day on which no work was to be done. But how are we to define the word *work*? What can and cannot be done on that day?

The Mishna identified 39 kinds of work not to be performed on the Sabbath, including sowing, reaping, spinning, sewing two stitches, hunting a gazelle, writing two letters, lighting a fire, carrying anything from one place to another, tying or untying knots.

Then the rabbis pondered: What is involved in tying a knot, and to what other human activities might this prohibition extend? They invited a sailor to discuss the matter with them and to demonstrate tying a knot. The sailor complied and, Michener observes,

129

after two months of discussion, Rabbi Asher proposed the following general rule: "Any joining together of two things that are by nature the same is equal to the tying of a knot." Thus, on Shabbat a man may not place additional grapes in a press which already contains grapes, for that is tying a knot.

p. 522

3. Marital Matters

A third subject under consideration was this: Under what circumstances may a Jewish person obtain a divorce? According to the Mishna, a person could divorce his or her spouse if the spouse was affected with a skin disorder (e.g., leprosy or boils), had a tumor of the nasal membranes that caused him or her to snore inordinately, or was a collector of manure.

The same section of the Mishna considers when a man can be free from having sexual relations with his wife:

> If one puts his wife under a vow to have no connubial relations, the school of Shammai said that this frees him for two weeks. The school of Hillel says one week. A student who goes forth to study the Law may be freed of connubial demands for a period of 30 days. A laborer may go for one week.

The Mishna also stipulated the frequency with which a man of independent means was to have marital relations with his wife: laborers, twice weekly; mule drivers, once a week; camel drivers, once every thirty days; sailors, once every six months. If the husband did not fulfill his obligation or if he was not satisfying his wife, then she could appeal to the Sanhedrin and be granted a divorce.

Other reasons the Mishna allowed for divorce: if the husband committed apostasy; if he contracted a loathsome disease; if he was impotent or unfaithful or refused to provide for her; if he was cruel to her mentally or physically. These interpretations help us understand what Jesus meant when He said: "You have heard it said, but I say. . . ."

Then the Gemara

As new and complicated questions arose, interpreters and commentators on the Torah competed for followers in the marketplace of ideas. Max I. Dimont in *Jews, God and History* comments:

> The first reinterpretation of Mosaic injunctions may have been based on nothing more than cleverness. But soon the interpreters were carried away by their own inventiveness. To outdo each other, they sought for profundity instead of mere ingenuity, and a new Biblical science was born.
>
> p. 167

Over the years, interpretations in the Mishna were further interpreted in the *Gemara* (which in Hebrew means "completion"), a supplement to the Mishna. Dimont says:

> Actually Gemara was nothing but warmed over Mishna, served orally in Aramaic, instead of in Hebrew, and disguised as amendments to the Mishna. A series of brilliant expounders elevated the Gemara to a status on a par with the Torah itself.
>
> p. 170

For the next several hundred years, work, study and discussion of both the Mishna and the Gemara continued. By about the sixth century C.E., both works were incorporated into a new work called the *Talmud*. The word *Talmud* comes from the Hebrew verb "to study." What the

131

people studied were commentaries on the written Law and the application of those commentaries to their lives.

The Awesome Complexity of the Talmud

The Talmud shaped rabbinic Judaism over the centuries. Yet at every twist and turn, it closes Jewish minds to the underlying principles of both the Tenach and the New Testament: the importance of faith. Why God chose the Jewish people. What a blood covenant is. The privileges and obligations of living in a blood covenant relationship with God. The attributes of God. And although most Jewish people today would not be able to distinguish between the Talmud and the latest Sidney Sheldon book, the Jewish community continues to follow certain practices originally laid out in the Talmud.

The Talmud fills fifteen thousand pages of writing contained in 35 volumes. It includes commentary on law and jurisprudence as well as ethics and morality. It deals with many phases of human life and touches on sciences such as medicine, hygiene, astronomy, economics and government. Remember, the Talmud required hundreds of years to compile and the efforts of countless scholars. Some of the greatest minds in Jewish history have labored over the issues of their daily lives and recorded what they felt were the ways to respond to those issues.

Please consider the enormity of what you have just read. Think about what *your* life would be like if this had been the primary set of books you read throughout your junior high and high school years, college and graduate school years. You could never absorb it all. There would always be more for you to learn, and always someone more educated than you on a given portion of the Talmud. Yet after many years of study, you might feel ready to teach some aspects of the Talmud to others.

132

Cinematic Views of the Talmud

Have you seen the films *Yentl* or *The Chosen*? If not, make a point to visit your local video store to rent them. I mention them because each contains wonderful scenes that show serious men of all ages deep in study. What were they studying? The Talmud.

In the movie *Yentl*, Barbra Streisand plays a young woman living decades ago in a tiny ghetto in Eastern Europe. She loved to watch the men as they studied the Talmud. She loved to hear them talk about it. She wanted desperately to study the Talmud herself. But she was a girl, and girls did not have that privilege. To solve her problem, she decided to masquerade as a boy so she would be permitted to study with the rabbi and the other *Talmudim* (students of the Talmud).

The other film, *The Chosen* (adapted from the novel by Chaim Potok), depicts two young Jewish boys growing up in Brooklyn. One is a Chasid, very Orthodox in his beliefs and actions. The other, although Orthodox, is much more liberal. What I remember best is the bearded, black-hatted rabbi teaching the Talmud to his students.

Part of my attraction to the film, I suppose, is that the learned rabbi reminds me so much of my grandfather, Isaac Baskin, who died at the age of 97. He was called Reb Isaac in the synagogue and was highly respected because he spent most of his life studying the Talmud. He never really learned to speak English and was not terribly learned in the social, political or economic events of twentieth-century America. But he knew a great deal about the Talmud.

One rabbi said this about a particular issue, Reb Isaac would reflect. But on the other hand, we have to remember what this other rabbi said. . . .

Do you remember the time the Pharisees asked Jesus, "Is it lawful for a man to divorce his wife for any and every reason?" (Matthew 19:3). Many miss what was happening here. Those Pharisees were doing what students of the Talmud normally do—query one another to find out which rabbinic tradition they followed.

Prior to the scene with Jesus, students of a Conservative rabbi learned that a man could divorce his wife only if he found some uncleanness in her. But there were Sadducees whose rabbis took a more liberal position. Those rabbis believed and taught that a man could put away his wife for any reason, so they came to Jesus to test Him. They wanted to know which rabbi He followed. Was He a Sadducee or a Pharisee?

Jesus, you will remember, did not get caught in that trap. He was not interested in what this or that rabbi said. He was interested in what God had declared in the Torah.

The Talmud Is Not the Tenach

We have reviewed two major historical events that caused the Jewish people to turn from the Tenach (the Jewish Scriptures): first, the destruction of the Temple, which led to the development of rabbinism and the teaching of salvation by works; and second, the development of the enormous body of law called the Talmud.

Most of the Jewish people you meet anywhere in the world today know almost nothing about the Bible, with the exception of the most familiar stories. And because they know almost nothing about the Bible, they know almost nothing about God.

In Israel, however, the situation is very different. The Tenach is studied throughout the nation, although it is studied primarily for its historical, geographical and archeological value. Only in some Israeli schools is it considered the Word of God to His chosen people, by which they are to live their lives. What a tremendous reminder to us that

> the man without the Spirit does not accept the things that come from the Spirit of God, for they are foolishness to him, and he cannot understand them, because they are spiritually discerned.
>
> 1 Corinthians 2:14

The wisdom of the Talmud is awesome, but it does not take the place of the Bible. Only in the Bible do we find instruction concerning the plan and purposes of God for His people. Only there do we learn of the New Covenant, and of the Messiah who was to come and whose blood would ratify that New Covenant.

For some Jewish people over the centuries, the Bible was replaced by the Talmud. Today, however, few Jews study the Talmud. For most of us Jews, the Bible has been replaced by the prayer book, a structured arrangement of traditional prayers and practices that are observed in the synagogue. As wonderful as these books are, neither the Talmud nor the prayer book contains the clear messianic prophecies that were fulfilled by the birth, life, death and resurrection of Jesus, our Messiah.

I end this chapter with a true story. I have changed only the names of the people involved.

A young Jewish GI in France during World War II fell in love with a charming French girl. After the war Bob and Colette married and moved to the United States. Periodically, however, they returned to Europe to visit Colette's family.

One year Colette's mom, who was not Jewish, was born again and set on fire for the Lord. That year the family was getting together near Geneva. She asked a local pastor to talk to Bob about the Lord. He agreed.

A few days later, when they were all together, Colette's mom invited the pastor over for lunch. Afterward he asked Bob to take a walk with him.

"Tell me, Bob," said the pastor as they walked, "what do you think about Jesus?"

"I don't," replied Bob. "I'm Jewish."

"Oh," said the pastor.

Long pause.

Then the pastor asked, "Bob, do you think Jesus is the Messiah?"

"Of course not," said Bob. "I told you, I'm Jewish."

Another long pause.

"Are you a student of the Old Testament?"

"No, I can't say I've ever really read it."

"Well, then," said the pastor, "have you ever read the New Testament?"

"Of course not. I told you, I'm Jewish."

Then the pastor said, "Let me see if I understand what you're telling me. You haven't read the Old Testament and you've never read the New. But you are absolutely convinced that Jesus is not the Jewish Messiah. Is that right?"

"Yes, that's right," said Bob.

"Well," said the pastor, "I must say, you form very strong opinions on no evidence, don't you?"

And with that he turned and left Bob with his mouth open.

We began this chapter with the question "What do today's Jews believe about God and the Bible?" Let's conclude it by recognizing that most of today's Jews rarely think of God. Some deny that He exists. Others think He is not relevant in today's society. Still others say that man is the only God on earth. Very few truly believe God is sovereign, omnipresent, omnipotent, omniscient, immutable and eternal.

Certainly Bob could not, with soaring spirit, declare with the apostle Paul,

> Oh, the depth of the riches of the wisdom and knowledge of God! How unsearchable his judgments, and his paths beyond tracing out! Who has known the mind of the Lord? Or who has been his counselor? Who has ever given to God, that God should repay him? For from him and through him and to him are all things. To him be the glory forever! Amen.
>
> Romans 11:33–36

As for what today's Jews think about the Bible, I would have to say that most are just like Bob: They don't think of it at all.

So how do we reach people like Bob with the Gospel? We will address that all-important question in chapter 12. But first let's get a better grasp of what today's Jewish people think about Jesus. We will consider this question in the next chapter.

What Do Today's Jews Think about Jesus?

Like Bob in our last chapter, most of us *don't* think about Jesus.

Oh, I suppose if you had pushed Bob, he might have said, "Yeah, sure, I know Jesus lived way back then. And obviously He was a good teacher. Or philosopher. He may even have been a prophet. But He was only a man. He wasn't God. And He certainly wasn't our Messiah!"

Are you beginning to see how complex a situation we face?

We saw in the last chapter that Jews—although they may be experts in science, medicine, government, art, literature, economics, law, psychology or sociology— know very little about the older Mosaic Covenant God made with Israel at Sinai or about the newer Covenant prophesied in Jeremiah. But the biggest tragedy is that most of us Jews know nothing about Jesus. We have formed very strong opinions on a subject about which most of us are, in the kindest sense of the word, ignorant.

When I was growing up, no one ever told me anything positive about Jesus. All I heard was that He is not for us. I didn't know why. All I knew was, "we" don't believe in Him. We are Jews!

Why can't Jews talk about Jesus or the New Testament? The simplest, most honest answer to that question is, "Because it's too threatening." It's better for us to avoid the New Testament and the claims of Jesus it contains. If those claims are true, we are in deep trouble. If we accepted them, we would also be admitting something about our ancestors—that they, too, were wrong. If we ignore Jesus, maybe He'll go away. It's better to ignore Him and say that that "Book" is not written to us and that it has no relevance for us. In that way we don't have to deal with what the New Covenant teaches.

On another level, most of us are ignorant about Jesus because we are ignorant about God. He is no longer the center of our lives. We don't understand what being in covenant relationship with Him means. We don't understand what the Mosaic Covenant has to do with our lives today. We don't know what it requires of us, or its blessings or cursings. (See chapter 10 for a fuller discussion of the blessings and cursings found in Deuteronomy 28.) We think the New Covenant is something Christians made up in order to discredit ours.

On still another level, we Jews take great comfort in hearing our rabbis quote Micah 6:8—"He hath showed thee, O man, what is good; and what doth the Lord require of thee, but to do justly, and to love mercy, and to walk humbly with thy God?" (KJV)—and we respond, "Great! That's easy enough. I can do that." We feel secure. If there *is* a God, we think, our concept of doing justly and loving mercy and walking humbly with Him is what matters and all that He requires of us.

Oh, how far we have strayed!

Those of us with more traditional backgrounds might recite twice daily the *Sh'ma*, the watchword of our faith: "Hear, O Israel: The LORD our God, the LORD is One!" (see Deuteronomy 6:4). We would then think, *See! We don't believe in three gods like the Christians. We have only one God.* And we would stick out our chests as we went about our business—completely ignoring the one God we had just professed.

I used to ride the BMT (Brooklyn-Manhattan Transit) subway into Manhattan each day. As the train rumbled across the Williamsburg Bridge, I saw a huge sign on the side of a building that read, *Believe on the Lord Jesus Christ and thou shalt be saved.* Each time I saw that sign I smirked.

How can believing something save you? I thought. *That's ridiculous! It's not what you believe that counts; it's what you do.*

A few years later I would say to myself, *What's all this about salvation? Saved from what? Maybe the Christians need to be saved from something, but we Jews don't!*

In view of our spiritual history as Jews, isn't it strange that most of us do not see God as our Creator? And isn't it surprising that we know so little about His covenants with us through Abraham and Moses? It's surprising, too, that we know so little about our Messiah.

What's a Messiah, Anyway?

In the spring of 1975, when I was trying to disprove the Messiahship of Jesus, I finally had to ask myself the question, "What's a Messiah?" I searched through some of the books I mentioned back in chapter 4 (including *A History of the Jews* by Abram L. Sachar and *Jews, God and History* by Max I. Dimont, as well as *My People* by Abba Eban). None of these books, I was surprised to learn, supplied information on what a Messiah is. Later I delved into Gerson Scholem's *Messianic Idea in Judaism* (Shocken, 1971), but was turned off when I realized it was written from a humanistic point of view.

This guy doesn't even believe in God! I thought. *How can he write about the Messiah?*

Then I came on Joseph Klausner's *Messianic Idea in Israel* (Macmillan, 1955) and began reading it with great anticipation. I sat up straight when I discovered that Klausner believed the Messiah would be a person. I was excited to read:

> The prophetic hope for the end of this age is one in which a strong redeemer, by his power and his spirit, will bring complete redemption, political and spiritual, to the people of Israel, and along with this, earthly bliss and moral perfection to the entire human race.

p. 9

What a statement!

As I read on, however, my frustration mounted. Through some five hundred pages, Klausner describes what different men have said about the prophecies contained in Scripture and how these opinions have been argued back and forth over the centuries. Some argued for a messianic person, others for a messianic age. But while the arguments raged, writes Klausner, one fact remained unchanged: "The Messianic idea is the most glistening jewel in the glorious crown of Judaism." That concept thrilled me, even though I did not yet believe in Jesus.

Is Klausner's conclusion about a Messiah shared by many Jewish people today? Many would say no. The ultra-Orthodox would say yes. Some of the most Orthodox still claim that Rabbi Menachem Mendel Schneerson, the Lubavitcher rabbi who died in 1994, is the Messiah.

Look at this copy from an ad that appeared in *Washington Jewish Week* on October 5, 1995 (notice that the name *God* is not spelled out, since that is considered taking the Lord's name in vain):

> The foundation of the belief of the Jewish people is the knowledge that there will be a time when the world will reach its intended perfection. A world of peace and harmony, without war, jealousy and greed. G-d will make this change through a great Jewish leader, known as the Moshiach [Messiah].

The ad went on to say that we Jews could bring "Messiah Schneerson" back. Unbelievable! How was this to be accomplished? We were to fill out a questionnaire, checking a series of choices under the title *I Want to Do Something Extra to Be Ready for Moshiach*, and return it to an address in Brooklyn, New York. The choices set before us included:

( ) Studying the Torah regularly;

( ) Giving my children a Jewish education;

( ) Purchasing new Torah books;

( ) Learning more about Moshiach;

( ) Lighting candles on the eve of every Shabbat [Sabbath] and holiday;

( ) Doing more to honor my parents;

( ) Putting on tefillin [phylacteries] every weekday;

( ) Putting up kosher mezuzahs [signposts] on my doorposts;

( ) Keeping kosher;

( ) Observing the laws of Jewish family life;

( ) Doing more to treat my neighbors kindly;
( ) Doing more to live in accordance with the Code of
    Jewish Law.

You can see, based on the above, that it is not the concept of a Messiah that causes so many Jews today to respond with anger and fear. Some probably smiled as they
read the above ad, but no one got upset because Rabbi
Schneerson was proclaimed the Jewish Messiah. Anger and
fear arise only when Jesus is named as the Jewish Messiah.

Squaring the Messianic Hope with Prophecy

For most of my life I did not know that the Hebrew
Scriptures contain dozens and dozens of prophecies—
about the Messiah's family line, about where He would
be born, about how He would grow up, about what He
would do when He came, about what would happen before He died. Daniel 9:26, written more than five centuries
before the coming of Jesus, even tells us when the Messiah would be killed.

Have you ever thought about the number of prophecies Jesus fulfilled? Jesus was:

Of the tribe of Judah
    Genesis 49:10   Hebrews 7:14; Revelation 5:5
Of the family line of Jesse
    Isaiah 11:1   Matthew 1:1; Romans 15:12
A prophet
    Deuteronomy 18:15 ff.   John 3:34; 6:14
A priest, but not from Levi
    Psalm 110:4   Hebrews 5:6; 6:20
A judge
    Isaiah 33:22   John 5:22; Acts 10:42

144

A king
    Psalm 2:6   1 Timothy 1:17; Revelation 15:3

Anointed by the Holy Spirit
    Isaiah 11:2   Matthew 3:16; John 1:32

Performing miracles
    Isaiah 35:5–6   Matthew 4:23–24; Luke 7:22

Teaching parables
    Psalm 78:2   Matthew 13:35

Betrayed by a friend
    Psalm 41:9   Matthew 26:23–25, 47–50

Sold for thirty pieces of silver
    Zechariah 11:12   Matthew 26:15

Forsaken by His disciples
    Zechariah 13:7   Matthew 26:31; Mark 14:27

Accused by false witnesses
    Psalm 35:11   Matthew 26:59–61

Unresponsive to His accusers
    Isaiah 53:7   Mark 14:61; 15:5; Luke 23:9

Wounded and bruised
    Isaiah 53:5   Mark 15:19; John 19:1–3

Smitten and spat upon
    Isaiah 50:6   Matthew 26:67; Mark 14:65

Mocked
    Psalm 22:6–8   Matthew 27:29–31; Mark 15:31–32

Pierced
    Zechariah 12:10   John 19:37; Revelation 1:7

Pierced in His hands and feet
    Psalm 22:16   Matthew 27:35; John 20:25–28

Hated by His own people
    Isaiah 53:3   Mark 15:29–30; Luke 23:23

Hated without reason
    Psalm 69:4   John 19:4, 6

Would suffer thirst
    Psalm 69:21   Matthew 27:34; John 19:28–29

Offered gall and vinegar
    Psalm 69:21   John 19:29

No bones broken
    Psalm 34:20   John 19:33

Buried with the rich
    Isaiah 53:9   Mark 15:43–46

In a section of a compilation entitled *Science Speaks* (Moody Press, 1963), Peter Stoner considers just eight of the above prophecies. His conclusion:

> We find that the chance that any man might have lived down to the present time and fulfilled all eight prophecies is one in ten to the 17th power. This would be 1 in 100,000,000,000,000,000. In order to help us comprehend this, we take 10 to the 17th power in silver dollars and lay them down on the face of Texas. They will cover the state two feet deep. Now mark one of these silver dollars and stir the whole mass thoroughly, all over the state. Blindfold a man and tell him that he can travel as far as he wishes, but he must pick up one silver dollar and say that this is the right one. What chance would he have of getting the right one? Just the same chance that the prophets would have had of writing just eight prophecies and having them all come true in any one man, from their day to the present time, providing they wrote them in their own wisdom.

Many Jews are threatened by this conclusion. Our rabbis say that we Jews who believe in Jesus think the way we do about these prophecies because we don't understand Hebrew and are misreading them.

In the synagogue we read none of these key Scriptures about the coming of our Messiah. It really does astound me to hear rabbis say that the clear prophecies that were fulfilled in Jesus' birth, life, death and resurrection are not convincing, and then turn around and admit that "Rabbi Schneerson might be the Messiah after all; we'll just have to wait and see."

I say with conviction, Rabbi Schneerson fulfilled none of the prophecies. Jesus fulfilled each of them.

Let's Not Forget the Subject of Sin

The subject of sin is another mystery. When we go to the synagogue, particularly on Rosh Hashanah (the Jewish New Year, the Feast of Trumpets) and Yom Kippur (the Day of Atonement), we read of sin in our prayer book. But many of us don't really understand what sinning against God means. The only kind of sin we know is sin against other human beings. And, like children, we think if we say we are sorry and promise never to do it again, God will forgive even our worst sins.

We ignore the subject of our accountability to God. Once we reach our teen years, we prefer to think we aren't accountable to anyone but ourselves. And if there is a sin in this life, it has to be the sin of getting caught!

No, we don't like to talk about sin. Nor have our rabbis taught us about our need for vicarious atonement from sin. Indeed, most of us are unfamiliar with what our ancient high priests did on the Day of Atonement in the Temple at Jerusalem (see Leviticus 16). We know almost nothing about the scapegoat sent into the wilderness each year at Yom Kippur. We are surprised, often open-mouthed, when we learn that our high priest used to collect the blood of a sacrificed lamb in a basin and carry it into the Holy of Holies so he could sprinkle it over the Mercy Seat and the Ark of the Covenant as he pleaded with God to forgive our sins.

The destruction of the Temple in the year 70 C.E. marked not only the end of the sacrificial system, but the beginning of a Judaism that ultimately saw no need for such a system at all.

What about Rosh Hashanah and Yom Kippur today? They are our two most observed Jewish holidays and come ten days apart in the early fall each year. The ten days between them are called "The Days of Awe." During this period, our tradition tells us, we are to examine our lives and repent of our sins. We are to be reconciled with all from whom we have been estranged. And we are to pray to God for forgiveness. If our prayers to God are earnest enough, on Yom Kippur God will forgive our sins and inscribe our names in His Book of Life for the next year.

One of the prayers read on Rosh Hashanah (taken from *The Union Prayerbook for Jewish Worship*, The Central Conference of American Rabbis, 1962) reads:

Praised be Thou, O Lord, God of our fathers, God of Abraham, Isaac and Jacob, great, mighty, and exalted. Thou bestowest lovingkindness upon all Thy children. Thou rememberest the devotion of the fathers. In Thy love, Thou bringest redemption to their descendants for the sake of Thy name. Remember us unto life, O King, who delightest in life, and inscribe us in the book of life, for Thy sake, O God of life. Thou art our King and Helper, our Savior and Protector. Praised be Thou, O Lord, Shield of Abraham.

p. 18

Note that the emphasis in this prayer is on God's relationship with Abraham, Isaac and Jacob, and that the plea for inclusion in the Book of Life is "for the sake of Thy name." Later in the service, we rise and read together:

Our Father, our King, hear our prayer.
Our Father, our King, we have sinned before Thee.

148

Our Father, our King, have mercy upon us and upon
  our children.
Our Father, our King, keep far from our country pesti-
  lence, war and famine.
Our Father, our King, cause all hate and oppression to
  vanish from the earth.
Our Father, our King, inscribe us for blessing in the
  book of life.
Our Father, our King, grant unto us a year of happiness.

pp. 28, 62

While synagogues all over the world may be mostly empty during the balance of the year, on Rosh Hashanah and Yom Kippur they are full.

I must tell you, I truly appreciate our prayer books. We have one that we use throughout the year and another one for Rosh Hashanah and Yom Kippur. The prayers contained in the prayer book for the high holy days are wonderful. The readings they suggest are inspired and touch our hearts. Consider:

What is man, O God, that Thou art mindful of him, and the son of man that Thou thinkest of him? How can mortal man appear pure and blameless before Thee in whose sight even the hosts of heaven are not perfect? How can he whose life is as a passing shadow account himself worthy to stand in Thy presence, O Thou Eternal One? Though we appear virtuous in the sight of men, yet who of us can stand before Thee who searchest the heart, to whom darkness is as light, and from whose eye nothing is hid? Thou are veiled from the eyes of all creatures; but their inmost ways lie open to Thee.

p. 210

Insightful words. Moving words. But do we Jews who read them really believe in the God of Abraham, Isaac and

149

Jacob and pray to Him as the covenant-giving and covenant-keeping God? Are we convinced He really hears us? Do we believe, in accordance with Jewish tradition, that He maintains three sets of books—one for the totally righteous, one for the totally unrighteous and one for those who are neither totally righteous nor totally unrighteous? Do we truly believe that if we pray hard enough, God will take our name from one book and inscribe it in the first book—the Book of Life?

Many Jews do believe in God. They believe they can pray to God for forgiveness and that He will forgive them and inscribe their names in the Book of Life for the next year. They leave the synagogue after the Yom Kippur service invigorated and relieved.

Many, many more of us, on the other hand, do not really believe these things. We join our fellow congregants in reciting the words of our prayers, but to us they seem little more than folklore. We see the concept of God's Book of Life and Book of Death as an ancient story that has little meaning today.

So if most of us Jews don't really believe in God or in the Hebrew Scriptures, why do we go to the synagogue on Rosh Hashanah and Yom Kippur? Why do many of us fast? Why do we send cards to one another that say, "May your name be inscribed in the Book of Life," if we don't really believe there *is* a Book of Life?

Perhaps because Yom Kippur is our main connection with our Jewishness.

What about the Covering of Our Sins?

I have already mentioned that, in lieu of the high priest's blood sacrifices and prayers for the covering of our sins, as described in Leviticus 16, we are taught that we can achieve our own right standing with God through prayer, study, charity and other good works. The more observant of us may go to the ocean or a river or even a running stream and cast bread, symbolizing our sins, into the water. As the water carries the bread away, never to return, we hope that our sins have been taken from us.

On Yom Kippur, we stand in the synagogue and recite these prayers (also from *The Union Prayerbook*):

> For the sin which we have sinned against Thee under
>   stress or through choice;
> For the sin which we have sinned against Thee openly
>   or in secret;
> For the sin which we have sinned against Thee in stub-
>   bornness or in error;
> For the sin which we have sinned against Thee in the
>   evil meditation of the heart;
> For the sin which we have sinned against Thee by word
>   of mouth;
> For the sin which we have sinned against Thee by
>   abuse of power;
> For the sin which we have sinned against Thee by the
>   profanation of Thy name;
> For the sin which we have sinned against Thee by dis-
>   respect for parents and teachers;
> For the sin which we have sinned against Thee by ex-
>   ploiting and dealing treacherously with one another;
> For all these sins, O God of forgiveness, bear with us!
>   Pardon us! Forgive us!
>
> pp. 148, 150

These are wonderful prayers. I have prayed them most sincerely, along with many others, for most of my life. Unfortunately, the recitation of wonderful and sincere prayers is not the complete way God says we obtain His forgiveness. Remember from Leviticus 16:14–17 and Leviticus 17:11 that it is blood that brings atonement (reconciliation between God and human beings) for sin. This principle was absolutely essential.

How do we respond when we read Leviticus 16–17 in the Torah today? We don't. We don't what? We don't read Leviticus 16–17, even though it is included as part of the weekly reading in the synagogue. In our private lives we say, "That was then; we don't do that anymore," or else we say, "Come on, you don't really believe that stuff, do you?"

Do Our Sins Require Payment?

I have recounted some of the prayers in which we ask God to forgive us our sins. I have also pointed out that prayer by itself cannot obtain forgiveness for us. Our sins can be covered for a time, if we follow God's procedure, but ultimately they have to be paid for.

I must also tell you that most of us Jews cannot conceive of having to pay for our sins. When we break God's Torah, we are taught that a prayer of confession will make everything right. But will it?

We know, of course, that when anyone in our country breaks the civil law, he or she is in trouble until the penalty for the crime is fully paid. But breaking God's law? Whoever had to pay personally for that kind of sin? Indeed, we cannot conceive of anyone actually paying for our sins. Most Jewish people don't have a clue as to why the death and resurrection of Jesus are so important.

In the synagogue, as I have said, we read none of the key Scriptures about the coming of our Messiah. Certainly we do not read Isaiah 53. When confronted by what it says, many of the rabbis I have spoken with explain that this portion of Isaiah speaks not of a Person taking on Himself the sins of human beings and being punished in their place, but of the Jewish people in general.

The next time you meet a messianic Jew, by contrast, ask him or her one of the following questions:

Why did Jesus come to earth the way He did, born of a Jewish virgin in Bethlehem?

What did He seek to accomplish by His wonderful deeds—walking on water, feeding five thousand, raising the dead, healing the sick?

Why did He make such staggering claims about Himself and His authority?

Why did He teach truths old and new—about being born again, about God's Kingdom, about commencing a personal relationship with God?

Why did He have to take to His own innocence all the sins and shame of the human race, making them His very own?

Why did He have to expose Himself to the judgment of God in our place?

In particular, ask a messianic Jew why Jesus' blood had to be shed and why His resurrection from the dead is so important.

But these truths about Jesus have almost no meaning to most Jewish people, apart from the terrible things that have been done to our people in His name. Some of us Jews may hunger for more information about our Messiah, but most of us have heard all we want to hear about "Christ"!

The Identity Problem Again

The problem as I saw it, before I became a follower of Jesus (and to many other Jewish minds as well), boiled down to our being who we were meant to be.

153

Let me make sure you understand what I mean. Most of us Jews believe we are who we were meant to be, so long as we remain Jewish. We also believe we will not be able to remain Jewish if we believe in your Jesus. That's why we stop listening to you every time you mention His name to us. We don't understand how a Jewish person can suddenly become one of Jesus' followers. How can you go east and west at the same time? How can you believe in Jesus and still be Jewish?

Listen to Jerome Chanes, co-director for domestic concerns for the National Jewish Community Advisory Council, addressing the issue of messianic Jews: "It is our view, position, that these people are misrepresenting themselves as Jews. They're not. They're Christians . . ." (*Washington Jewish Week*, May 23, 1996).

Remember the major misconception we Jewish people hold about Christians. It has to do with the Hebrew word *goyim*, which means "nations." In English the word *goyim* is translated "Gentiles." Remember that God created all the people of the world—all the Gentiles. Then, in the fullness of time, God chose one of those Gentiles, Abram, and through him, along with his sons Isaac and Jacob, established the Jewish people. If you are a Jew, you cannot be a Gentile. And if you are a Gentile, you cannot be a Jew. Yes, you can convert to Judaism, but the only way you can become a Jew is to be born of Jewish parents or be born of a convert to Judaism. Those are facts.

Today, however, most Jewish people do not think in terms of Jews and Gentiles. We think of Jews and Christians. If you are one, so we think, you cannot be the other.

Recall the situation in Israel that I wrote about in chapter 6. Israel is willing to grant citizenship under the Law of Return to almost every person in the world of Jewish ancestry, even people with only one Jewish grandparent—even if they deny the very existence of the God of

Abraham, Isaac and Jacob. But the present government, by decree of the Supreme Court of Israel just a few years ago, is unwilling to grant citizenship to Jewish men and women who love the God of Abraham, Isaac and Jacob and who believe Jesus is the Messiah God sent to restore Israel to Himself! These believers cannot receive Israeli citizenship under the Law of Return because, ostensibly, they are no longer Jews.

To many Jews, accepting Jesus means that despite your Jewish parentage, you have become a Gentile.

It's an astonishing conclusion, isn't it? It points out the powerful spiritual forces at work. Satan has been very successful in convincing the Jewish people of a terrible lie: that if a Jewish person accepts Jesus as Lord of his life, he becomes a Christian, forfeits his Jewishness and joins the enemies of the Jewish people.

But this fear—that if we Jews accept Jesus, we will no longer be Jewish—is irrational. Think about it. How did we get to be Jews in the first place? We were born of Jewish parents. Can that process be reversed? Can we become unborn? Even the Talmud states, "Once a Jew, always a Jew."

So, I ask, has God changed His mind? Has He declared that we Jews who believe in Jesus are no longer Jews? Who in this world has the power or authority to take our blood line and heritage from us? No one.

What Happened in 1967

In 1967 Jerusalem was restored to Jewish sovereignty, fulfilling a prophecy of Jesus: "Jerusalem will be trampled on by the Gentiles until the times of the Gentiles are fulfilled" (Luke 21:24).

Many Christians all over the world are convinced that "the times of the Gentiles" are fulfilled now, with the end of Gentile control of Jerusalem, and that God is drawing Jewish people to Himself in a powerful way.

The restoration of Jerusalem into Jewish hands for the first time in two thousand years triggered a spiritual phenomenon that is almost beyond comprehension. Since then more and more of us Jews are overcoming our fear of losing our identities and are accepting Jesus as our Messiah. Many thousands of Jewish people all over the world have seen through the lies of Satan and are finding and proclaiming Jesus as Messiah, Savior and Lord. Most of us like being called messianic Jews to emphasize that we have not stopped being Jews.

The latest estimate I have is that there are more than six thousand Jewish believers living in Israel today, and more than 85 congregations serving them. Try telling one of them that he or she is no longer Jewish and see how far you get.

In every major city in the United States, as well as in Europe, South America, South Africa, the former Soviet Union, Australia, Canada—wherever there are large percentages of Jewish people—you will find Jewish believers in Jesus. And although there is no way to verify the exact number, it has been estimated that Jewish believers in the United States today number between eighty and one hundred thousand.

So What Do Today's Jews Think about Jesus?

I cannot tell you, of course, what each and every one of today's Jews think about Jesus. But I can tell you what *I* think about Him.

Despite my love for Jewish culture and people, despite my unquestioned *yiddishkeit* (Jewishness), the reality is that my identity is not in my Jewishness. Oh, I love being Jewish—I've told you that already. Maybe it's like someone else loves being Irish or being a Southerner. But ethnic or regional identity is not the identity I am speaking about. I am speaking of spiritual identity.

Jesus is the Lord of my life. My true identity is in Him. I am a new creation. It is in Jesus that I live and move and have my being. I am complete in Him. And it is Jesus who is to be exalted in everything and by everything I do. The mystery that has been hidden from all ages is now revealed. The Messiah in me is my hope of glory. The life I live in my body, I live depending on the faithfulness of the Son of God in me. He loved me and gave Himself for me.

In the statements you have just read (all of them from Scripture), I have declared the central truth of my life. Please know that more and more Jewish people all over the world are now able to join me in saying, "I stand on the Word of God and proclaim that neither the Jewish community nor the rabbis of this world nor the State of Israel made me Jewish, and none of them can take my Jewish identity from me." Numerically we are still a significant minority within the Jewish community worldwide, but our numbers are increasing every day.

What about those other Jewish people—the ones who do not yet know Jesus? We will focus on them in the third section of this book, "Questions You Are Now Ready to Ask."

PART

3

Questions You Are Now Ready to Ask

Do the Jewish people really need Jesus? If they do, what is the best way to reach them? What does the Church need to know? And what does the Church need to do?

In Part 3 of this book we will answer these questions.

10

Do the Jewish People Really Need Jesus?

When my friends in Jews for Jesus go out onto the streets to distribute their "broadside" leaflets, they have two aims in mind. First, they want to bring every person face to face with the good news that God is a loving and seeking God, and that He has sent Jesus into the world to be their Savior and Friend. I rejoice with them as they achieve this goal. But why, some ask, do they have to wear T-shirts with *Jews for Jesus* printed boldly on them?

It points up their second aim: to remind everyone who sees them that Jesus is for Jews as well as for non-Jews. My friends feel obligated to challenge the terrible lie believed both in and out of churches and especially in synagogues— that Jesus is not for the Jewish people, and that Jews don't really need Him.

In many churches today you get the impression that sharing the

Gospel with Jewish people was never part of God's plan. Jesus, these churchgoers imply, is only for Gentiles.

I warned in the preface that if you don't believe in God, you will probably not enjoy reading many parts of this book. If you don't believe the Bible is God's Word, then what I am about to say in this chapter may not interest you. (It may even repulse you.) And if you don't believe Jesus is the Messiah whose coming was prophesied throughout the Hebrew Scriptures, then you have not been able to grasp what you've read.

If, on the other hand, you believe in the God of Abraham, Isaac and Jacob, and that the Bible is God's Word, and that Jesus is God's Messiah sent to earth to take our sins on Himself so we can be restored to Him, then you will fully comprehend what you are about to read.

It's the answer to that all-important question, Do Jewish people really need Jesus?

Objective versus Subjective Truth

In September 1954 I had just turned thirty. Ethel and I were about to celebrate our daughter Judy's first birthday. And we had just purchased our first home. It cost $17,750 and we bought it with no money down on a four percent GI loan. At the time I was earning $8,500 a year working as an account executive for a public relations firm. You may smile at this next statement, but I was really concerned about our ability to handle the mortgage. Together with real estate taxes it totaled $109 per month.

With the new house, we were starting a new phase in our lives. We decided it was time to join a synagogue.

So, a week before Rosh Hashanah, I walked a block and a half down the street to a Conservative synagogue, filled out a membership card for our family and made a pledge to the building fund—all without having attended a single service.

A week later, after the first night of the holiday, I knew I had made a mistake. While the rabbi was probably a fine man away from the pulpit, he had a tongue like a cat-o'-nine tails when he addressed the congregation. He was whipping everybody. That took care of that! I was not about to be whipped by anyone. Even more quickly than I had decided to join the congregation, I decided to unjoin.

During the next few months we visited different congregations, including a Reform temple about which we had heard good things. The rabbi there was young and dynamic. His congregation lacked the warmth and ritual I remembered from my youth, but the services were almost entirely in English. What I would lose in nostalgia, I figured, I would make up in understanding.

Also, I liked the way the rabbi put things. The first time I heard him speak, he had this to say:

"Some people come to temple because they're lonely or they're looking for business or looking for understanding or looking for a husband or a wife or looking for a new identity. I don't care why you come, but come. And let's pray and hope that together we will find God."

This was my kind of guy! He was intelligent and inquisitive. Apparently he hadn't found God yet either, so there was hope for me.

In order to get a better fix on Judaism, I decided to take the rabbi's course on comparative religions. The first Monday night we met, there were about twelve people in the class. The rabbi began by asking a crucial question—so crucial that I have never forgotten it.

"If all memory of organized religion were suddenly to be obliterated from the face of the earth overnight," he asked, "no more synagogues, no more churches, no more Bibles or prayer books—what would happen?"

Silence descended on us. All of us were thinking.

Then someone offered, "Without any form of religion, we'd have chaos. There would be no basis for law or contracts or marriage or any interpersonal relationships at all."

We soon agreed that eventually people would begin to ask questions: *Where did I come from? Where did you come from? Who created the universe? Is there a God? How do I communicate with Him, or He with me?*

Then the rabbi pointed out that although these questions would be asked all over the world, different people would come up with different answers.

"And that's the way it should be," he concluded. "Everyone is entitled to his opinion, right?"

Every head in the room went up and down. "Right. That's the way it should be."

And with that as a base, the rabbi introduced us to the study of comparative religions.

Many decades have passed since I took that class, but I remember clearly what happened that night because it made such an impression on me. The rabbi was saying that since everything is relative, the opinions of us Jews are as valid as anyone else's.

It sounds good, doesn't it? And from a secular point of view, he had a point. But the rabbi had confused subjective truth with objective truth. Here's what I mean. Truth defined by opinion alone is subjective truth. But truth that is truth despite anyone's opinion is objective truth.

The rabbi, whether he knew it or not, had laid a trap for us. He had established a false basis for our discussion. He had us presuppose that if all memory of organized religion were obliterated from the face of the earth, then what anyone thought about truth would be true. But his presupposition was contrary to fact. Available to each one of us is the record of all God has done—a record that can never be obliterated. "In the past God spoke to our forefathers through the prophets at many times and in various ways" (Hebrews 1:1). Neither this rabbi nor anyone else can discard objective reality.

A Potentially Fatal Error

So let's restate our chapter question: Do the Jewish people really need Jesus?

If you had asked me this question back in 1954, when I was taking that comparative religions class, I probably would have answered, "Sure, we need Jesus. Like we need a hole in our heads! Or like we need a good case of terminal cancer. Why don't you Christians leave us alone? You have your God and we have ours. We don't need your Jesus!"

That's what I would have said then. Today, by the grace of God, the scales have dropped from my eyes and I can see. Accordingly I am able to agree with God: The Jewish people of the world *do* need Jesus. They may not want or accept Him, but no one except Jesus can take care of our sins and restore us to God.

What *I* say on this subject, however, must not be what motivates you to belief or action. You have to be convinced from evidence that you yourself consider.

So let me ask you the question: Do *you* believe the Jewish people need Jesus? Do you believe it is really necessary for the Gospel to be preached to them today?

Many say the Church ought to leave the Jews alone. We looked in chapter 2 at some of the unscriptural thinking that abounds: "A person born Jewish should not seek to become a Christian." "Jews have suffered enough." "They don't need the New Covenant; they already have a covenant relationship with almighty God."

Possibly those who feel that the Jewish people don't need Jesus because of "their existing Mosaic covenant with God" don't really understand what a blood covenant is. They may not understand that it is the most binding of all agreements.

Let me tell you about a man I met recently. Let's call him Harvey. A friend of mine named Peter, who had been witnessing to Harvey, asked me to join the two of them for lunch one day at a restaurant called Bread and Chocolate on upper Connecticut Avenue in Washington, D.C. Both Peter and Harvey are Jewish. Peter, who is in his mid-thirties, had told Harvey, who is in his mid-seventies, a little bit about me, even as he had told me a little bit about Harvey. We both looked forward to meeting one another.

After we ordered lunch, I asked Harvey to tell me about himself. He was more than happy to do so. Born and raised in Washington, D.C., a graduate of Central High School, he had been in real estate sales for many years. Two years ago his wife died and now he was seeing a wonderful woman "who happens to be a Baptist lady."

"I told her that her religion was her concern," he said, "but that she would be wasting her time if she tried to convert me."

"How so?" I replied.

"I'm an atheist."

"Oh? Have you studied enough to be an atheist, or is it just a feeling with you?"

"What do you mean?"

"Well, you can spend a lot of time studying atheism, and then, based on what you've studied, come to the conclusion that God doesn't exist. Or you can just choose to believe God doesn't exist without any study at all. Which way did you follow?"

Harvey was thoughtful for a moment. His eyes were fixed on me. My eyes didn't waver as I waited for his response.

Finally he said with a laugh, "Oh, I didn't have to do any study. I just knew it inside of me."

"I didn't feel the way you feel when I was a kid," I said. "I just wasn't sure there is a God. I guess you'd have called me an agnostic."

"Hmm."

"Tell me, Harvey, have you ever read the Bible?"

"Can't say that I have."

"Do you know anything about the covenants God cut with us?"

"What do you mean?"

"I mean the covenant God cut with Abraham and the one He cut with Moses. The covenants in which God bound Himself to us as a people and under which we are bound to God."

"Oh, I guess I read about those when I was growing up," he said. "But they don't mean anything to me now. I don't believe that stuff."

You don't have to be a rocket scientist to know that I had my work cut out for me. I didn't think Harvey was open to hearing what I am about to say to you, so I didn't say it to him.

But the objective truth of the matter is this: Whether a Jewish person believes in God or not changes nothing. Our unbelief does not affect God's being or His deity or His power or His covenantal promises. He is God. The same thing can be said about a person who doesn't believe in George Washington. Someone's unbelief changes none of the facts about George Washington's life or the fact that he was our first president.

God is the great "I Am." Scripture does not attempt to prove this truth. It is a given. The Bible starts, "In the beginning God." In other words, God is. He is our God not because we are great or mighty or powerful or because we deserve for Him to be our God. And He established His covenant with the descendants of Abraham, Isaac and Jacob while we were the fewest of all peoples (see Deuteronomy 7:6–7). As an act of God's grace, He declared that He would be our God and that we would be His chosen people.

God bound Himself to us in His covenants with us. And we are bound by these covenants whether we know it or not, whether we like it or not.

Blessings and Curses of the Covenant

In the Mosaic covenant, God set forth 613 commandments that we are to keep all the days of our lives. If we obey them, He will bestow many blessings on us. If we do not obey them, then manifold curses will be on our heads and the heads of our children.

Rather than try to explain to you the blessings and cursings God ordained, I would like you to read God's Word for yourself. The first seven verses of Deuteronomy 28 (NKJV) list some of the wonderful blessings that will be ours if we keep all God's 613 commandments:

"Now it shall come to pass, if you diligently obey the voice of the LORD our God, to observe carefully all His commandments which I command you today, that the LORD your God will set you high above all nations of the earth.

"And all these blessings shall come upon you and overtake you, because you obey the voice of the LORD your God:

"Blessed shall you be in the city, and blessed shall you be in the country.

"Blessed shall be the fruit of your body, the produce of your ground and the increase of your herds, the increase of your cattle and the offspring of your flocks.

"Blessed shall be your basket and your kneading bowl.

"Blessed shall you be when you come in, and blessed shall you be when you go out.

"The LORD will cause your enemies who rise against you to be defeated before your face; they shall come out against you one way and flee before you seven ways."

The list of blessings goes on for a full fourteen verses. Aren't they amazing?

Then come 54 verses of cursings that will be upon our heads if we break any of God's 613 commandments. Here is a brief sampling of the cursings (with verse numbers in front of them so you can find them in your own Bible):

15. But it shall come to pass, if you do not obey the voice of the LORD your God, to observe carefully all His commandments and His statutes which I command you today, that all these curses will come upon you and overtake you:

16. "Cursed shall you be in the city, and cursed shall you be in the country.

17. "Cursed shall be your basket and your kneading bowl.

18. "Cursed shall be the fruit of your body and the produce of your land, the increase of your cattle and the offspring of your flocks.

19. "Cursed shall you be when you come in, and cursed shall you be when you go out.

20. "The LORD will send on you cursing, confusion, and rebuke in all that you set your hand to do, until you are destroyed and until you perish quickly, because of the wickedness of your doings in which you have forsaken Me.

24. "The LORD will change the rain of your land to powder and dust; from the heaven it shall come down on you until you are destroyed.

25. "The LORD will cause you to be defeated before your enemies; you shall go out one way against them and flee seven ways before them; and you shall become troublesome to all the kingdoms of the earth.

29. "And you shall grope at noonday, as a blind man gropes in darkness; you shall not prosper in your ways; you shall be only oppressed and plundered continually, and no one shall save you.

32. "Your sons and your daughters shall be given to another people, and your eyes shall look and fail with long-

ing for them all day long; and there shall be no strength in your hand.

33. "A nation whom you have not known shall eat the fruit of your land and the produce of your labor, and you shall be only oppressed and crushed continually.

36. "The LORD will bring you and the king whom you set over you to a nation which neither you nor your fathers have known, and there you shall serve other gods—wood and stone.

37. "And you shall become an astonishment, a proverb, and a byword among all nations where the LORD will drive you.

45. "Moreover all these curses shall come upon you and pursue and overtake you, until you are destroyed, because you did not obey the voice of the LORD your God, to keep His commandments and His statutes which He commanded you.

47. "Because you did not serve the LORD your God with joy and gladness of heart, for the abundance of everything,

48. "therefore you shall serve your enemies, whom the Lord will send against you, in hunger, in thirst, in nakedness, and in need of everything; and He will put a yoke of iron on your neck until He has destroyed you.

49–50. "The LORD will bring a nation against you from afar, from the end of the earth, as swift as the eagle flies, a nation whose language you will not understand, a nation of fierce countenance, which does not respect the elderly nor show favor to the young.

62. "You shall be left few in number, whereas you were as the stars of heaven in multitude, because you would not obey the voice of the LORD your God.

66. "Your life shall hang in doubt before you; you shall fear day and night, and have no assurance of life.

67. "In the morning you shall say, 'Oh, that it were evening!' And at evening you shall say, 'Oh, that it were morning!' because of the fear which terrifies your heart, and because of the sight which your eyes see."

Can you see aspects of the Holocaust in what you have just read?

I have often told people that if they want to remain wide awake some night, they should read the entire 28th chapter of Deuteronomy and consider that the curses promised there await them personally. But they shouldn't stop with Deuteronomy 28. Since everything is to be established out of the mouths of two or three witnesses, they should also read Exodus 23:20–33 and Leviticus 26. Finally they should see how God, speaking through Moses, summarizes His position:

> This day I call heaven and earth as witnesses against you that I have set before you life and death, blessings and curses. Now choose life, so that you and your children may live.
>
> Deuteronomy 30:19

To the Jewish people the challenge is clear: We Jews will obey God, be blessed and live, or else we will disobey God, be cursed and die. This is not subjective truth. It is objective reality.

What's at Stake: The Covenant of Grace

Now let me stress a tragic fact: I do not believe there is a Jewish person on the face of the earth who even *knows* the 613 commandments of the Law. So how can we possibly keep them? Does this mean that the curses of Deuteronomy 28 await all Jewish people throughout the world unless they are delivered from them? Precisely. And there is only one way by which they can be delivered.

With that conviction compelling me, I exhort you, in the name of the Lord, to think about the Jewish people you know. Recognize that they do not realize what awaits them. They do not fully understand the significance of God's covenant with them. They do not comprehend that the curses of God are real and that there is no way to escape them through their own efforts. No matter how educated they become. No matter how much they give to charity. No matter how many Nobel prizes they win. No matter how large their contribution to society. They still must face almighty God and bear responsibility for the commands of God that they have broken.

I trust you understand by now that the vast majority of Jewish people know very little of God, of His Word, of His covenants and of His grace. So please reread the story of Lazarus and the rich man in Luke 16:19–31 and let God's compassion for the Jewish people rise within you. If you love any of them, if you have any heart for them, if you would like to see them saved from the wrath of God, then begin praying for them. Pray that God will send laborers to bring them the covenant of grace under which they can be saved from those curses.

But be prepared to put feet to your prayers by becoming such a laborer yourself. If you do not share God's truth with the Jewish people you know, who will?

The Real Anti-Semitism

I believe with all my heart that the most anti-Semitic thing a Bible-believing Christian can do to the Jewish people is deny them access to the good news of Messiah Jesus.

Think of Jesus' claim that He did "not come to abolish [the Law or the Prophets] but to fulfill them" (Matthew 5:17). This does not mean only that He came into the world as a Jewish man and obeyed every one of the 613 laws of God. There is more to it than that. He also never had it in His heart to disobey any of those laws. After all,

God does not judge only the overt act of sinning, but regards even our toleration of the impulse toward disobedience as sin. Jesus taught,

> "What comes out of a man is what makes him 'unclean.' For from within, *out of men's hearts,* come evil thoughts, sexual immorality, theft, murder, adultery, greed, malice, deceit, lewdness, envy, slander, arrogance and folly."
>
> Mark 7:20–22 (my emphasis)

Jesus Himself embodied the perfect righteousness of God. And the Bible tells us that "without holiness no one will see the Lord" (Hebrews 12:14). Unless a man or woman can say that God "has . . . arrayed me in a robe of righteousness" (Isaiah 61:10), what hope does he or she have of standing in His presence?

Which brings us to the matter of our guilt and shame for having disobeyed God in thought, word and deed. What solution has Messiah Jesus brought to this awful predicament? The solution is found in the cross.

Even before we can be arrayed in God's righteousness, we read that we must be cleansed of our defilement. The prophet Isaiah wrote, surely with the cross in mind, that the Messiah "was pierced for our transgressions, he was crushed for our iniquities" (53:5–6) and that "he bore the sin of many" (verse 12). What can we conclude? That by accepting Jesus as Messiah and Lord, we Jews will be saved from the horrible curses of Deuteronomy 28 and the wrath of God against sin.

But many Christians want to be politically correct. When they go to the hospital to visit a Jewish friend, they do not want to offend that person by talking about Jesus. I have often wondered how they feel when the Jewish friend they never told about Jesus dies.

Our pride and willingness to be disobedient to God are two of the major forces behind our self-consciousness and fear of speaking the truth. These motivations make us useless to God and will be judged for the sins they are. We must repent of them and seek by God's grace to be indifferent to public opinion. Sensitive to the special needs of Jewish people? Of course. We will look at that further in chapter 13. But silent Christians? That is hardly what God wants us to be!

Revisiting the Apostle Paul

Further, we must not forget that God has a plan and mission for the Jewish people. Our faithful sharing of the Gospel is related to their becoming central once again in the worldwide purposes of God. Recall the observation made by the apostle Paul:

> Again I ask: Did they stumble so as to fall beyond recovery? Not at all! Rather, because of their transgression, salvation has come to the Gentiles to make Israel envious.
>
> Romans 11:11

Then Paul focuses his comments:

> I am talking to you Gentiles. Inasmuch as I am the apostle to the Gentiles, I make much of my ministry in the hope that I may somehow arouse my own people to envy and save some of them.
>
> verses 13–14

Later he expresses his heartfelt conviction:

> If they do not persist in unbelief, they will be grafted in, for God is able to graft them in again. After all, if you were cut out of an olive tree that is wild by nature, and contrary to nature were grafted into a cultivated olive tree, how much more readily will these, the natural branches, be

174

grafted into their own olive tree! I do not want you to be ignorant of this mystery, brothers, so that you may not be conceited: Israel has experienced a hardening in part until the full number of the Gentiles has come in. And so all Israel will be saved, as it is written: "The deliverer will come from Zion; he will turn godlessness away from Jacob."

verses 23–26

Now that Jerusalem is once again in Jewish hands, "the times of the Gentiles" (Luke 21:24) are being fulfilled. It is time to show favor to Zion (see Psalm 102:13). It is time to bring the good news of Messiah Jesus to the Jewish people.

What Do *You* Believe?

What do you understand from Scripture?

If you were Jewish, would you want to experience the curses of God or the wrath that is to come? Would you want your parents to experience it? Your children? Your brothers and sisters? The people you love? Your neighbors? Your doctor? Your accountant? Your storekeeper? Your insurance man? Wouldn't you want someone to tell you how these horrors can be avoided?

God does not want anyone to experience His wrath. The apostle Peter declared this about the judgment:

The Lord is not slow in keeping his promise, as some understand slowness. He is patient with you, not wanting *anyone* to perish, but everyone to come to repentance.

2 Peter 3:9 (my emphasis)

God wants all Jewish people to be redeemed from these curses and to receive eternal life.

But His grace is not limited to the Jewish people:

175

> For God so loved the world that he gave his one and only Son, that *whoever* believes in him shall not perish but have eternal life. For God did not send his Son into the world to condemn the world, but to save the world through him.
>
> John 3:16–17 (my emphasis)

That is God's will, and it includes salvation for the Jewish people.

What is *your* will? Is it your will to do God's will? Are you willing to do whatever you can to bring the Gospel to the Jews? To work with others to bring about what God wants done? Jewish people must accept or reject Jesus on an individual basis. But how can they make informed decisions if they have not heard or do not understand the Gospel? As Paul wrote, in the context of Jewish evangelism:

> How, then, can they call on the one they have not believed in? And how can they believe in the one of whom they have not heard? And how can they hear without someone preaching to them?
>
> Romans 10:14

In obedience to almighty God, each of us is responsible to share the Gospel with all who are willing to hear— "first . . . the Jew, then . . . the Gentile" (see Romans 1:16; 2:9–10). We are required to be obedient to the Great Commission (see Matthew 28:18–20) and work together to accomplish God's will.

I say these things to you not to spread condemnation. God forbid! Rather, my prayer is that you will recognize the urgency of the need and be motivated to act.

Which of us would hesitate to warn our Jewish neighbors if we knew their apartment building was on fire? Would we refuse to tell them about the flames roaring in the basement below and rushing toward their floor—perhaps because they had dinner guests and shouldn't be disturbed?

Without Jesus the Jewish people are without hope in the world. This is the Word of God.

In the next chapter I want to offer a change of pace, tell a story and then let my granddaughter raise an intriguing question.

At the Heart of the Matter

I want to tell you a true story about my family. The star of the story is my granddaughter Jennifer, who asked her mother an important question one Sunday morning after church. It illustrates a problem many Jewish believers have with their families and points to a scriptural truth about Jewish people today.

Jennifer and her mom and dad lived near us in suburban Washington, D.C. Judy and her husband had accepted Jesus as Messiah and Lord. And just before Jennifer's fifth birthday, she had asked Jesus to come into her heart, too. As she continued to grow, she had no doubt about two things: She was Jewish and Jesus was Lord of her life.

Jennifer, her parents and our other daughter, Ann, all attended the Living Word Fellowship, the church I pastored. It was a blessing

179

for Ethel and me to worship the Lord each week with our family.

And on each of the three major Jewish holidays—Rosh Hashanah, Yom Kippur and Passover—our entire family came together. Ethel prepared fantastic meals, and the joy level at our table was full to overflowing.

Our Passover Seder

In 1984 the Passover Seder (service) fell on a Saturday night, a few weeks before Jennifer's sixth birthday. Ethel did her usual outstanding job preparing for the holiday. The house sparkled. Joining us that year were Ethel's older sister, Bess, and her husband, Joe, who were visiting from Florida. Neither Bess nor Joe believed in Jesus. Also joining us was Heidi, a radiant believer from Recife, Brazil, who had been our beloved housekeeper for many years.

Everyone arrived wearing their best clothes. There was much laughter and hugging. Aromas from the wonderful dinner Ethel was preparing for us filled the house.

Thirty minutes before dinner, it was time to begin the first part of our Seder. (It would conclude after dinner.)

When each person was seated, Ethel lit the two white candles in tall, freshly polished silver candlesticks given to us as wedding presents 34 years before. She prayed the traditional Hebrew prayer over them. Then I distributed copies of the same *Haggadah* (the book containing the order of the service and story of Passover) that I had used for our family service before we became messianic Jews.

The Seder began when I dipped my hands into a silver bowl filled with water, then rinsed and dried them using a white linen towel. Next I recited the *Kiddush*, a prayer of thanksgiving to God for choosing us as His people and making it possible for us to celebrate this festive meal together. Then I called everyone's attention to the special Passover plate before me. One by one I lifted up each of the items on the plate and explained its significance to us as Jews.

I began with the roasted hard-boiled egg on which my wife had placed burn marks from a lit match.

"This egg," I explained, "reminds us of two things. First, since it has no beginning or end, it reminds us of what our lives will be like when we are with God. We will spend eternity with Him. There will be no end for us. Also, the burn marks on the outside shell of the egg remind us of the destruction of our Temple in Jerusalem two thousand years ago."

Then I lifted up a plate containing *haroses*, a mixture of apples, chopped nuts, raisins and wine.

"We were slaves in Egypt for more than four hundred years," I went on. "During those years we made bricks and mortar for Pharaoh's store cities. The haroses reminds us of the mortar we were forced to prepare—day after day, week after week, month after month, year after year. It was very hard work."

Next from the Seder plate I lifted a little plate filled with *maror*, bitter herbs, reminding us how bitter our lives had been when we were slaves in Egypt. Then a small cup of salt water, reminding us of the tears we had shed as slaves. And the parsley to be dipped into the salt water reminded us that so long as there is life, there is hope, even in the midst of our tears.

Finally I took from the Passover plate the shankbone of a lamb and held it up.

"This shankbone reminds us of God's provision and special protection at that first Passover Seder," I said, looking around the table. "He commanded that every Hebrew household in Egypt seek out a year-old lamb without blemish and keep it for four days. Then, long before sundown, it was to be killed and its blood placed on the two doorposts and the lintel of the entrance to the house. Then the lamb was roasted so that every member of the household might eat it that night. No one was to leave the house after dinner until the next morning, because the angel of death would slay the firstborn in every Egyptian family that night, but 'pass over' our homes that had been marked with the blood of the lamb."

Then we proceeded to read through the Haggadah. A few moments later Jennifer read the questions traditionally asked by the youngest person at the table:

"Why is this night different from all other nights? On all other nights, we eat either leavened or unleavened bread. Why, on this night, do we eat only unleavened bread?

"On all other nights, we eat all kinds of herbs. Why, on this night, do we eat especially bitter herbs?

"On all other nights, we do not dip herbs in any condiment. Why, on this night, do we dip them in salt water and haroses?

"On all other nights, we eat without special festivities. Why, on this night, do we hold this Seder service?"

As the service continued, each person old enough to read took a turn in reading aloud from the Haggadah as the story unfolded. As we heard the story once again, I looked lovingly around the table. The faces looked at times somber, at times joyous, reflecting gratitude for God's faithfulness and deliverance of our Jewish people.

But I was concerned about Bess and Joe. How were they reacting to our Seder? Since I was using the same Haggadah we had used before we became believers, which made no mention of Jesus, I was fairly sure they would be comfortable with it. But I would be speaking at the end of the Seder about the relationship between the Passover meal, Jesus' Last Supper and His establishment of the New Covenant. I knew, too, that we would share the matzo and wine of Communion. I didn't know how they would respond to that.

When the first part of our Seder was over, everyone was more than ready to experience the wonders Ethel had been preparing all day. We had *gefilte* fish, a delectable combination of white fish and yellow pike, eggs, onions and matzo meal (either chopped or ground) shaped like large, flattened meatballs. (This is normally served with horseradish). Then Ethel served her very special chicken soup with the lightest matzo balls. Roast turkey and brisket of beef followed, with all kinds of side dishes. We had plates full of regular matzo (unleavened bread prepared specially for Passover) as well as egg matzo (a different kind of matzo). Ethel also prepared *chullunt*, an unbelievable mixture of prunes, carrots, sweet potatoes and other mysterious ingredients that had been cooked and cooked until receiving her final O.K. We enjoyed tossed salad and plates full of celery, carrots, olives and pickles.

When dinner was over and the table was cleared, dessert plates were brought out. There was honey cake and sponge cake and fruit cake, different kinds of macaroons (my favorites are chocolate-covered), fresh strawberries and assorted nuts, along with stewed, dried fruit and loads of special Passover candies. Then came coffee and tea.

Dinner was absolutely wonderful! It took much longer to eat our dinner than it did to read through the first part of the Seder. But when dinner was over, we continued with the rest of that blessed Passover Seder.

Although Bess and Joe were with us, there was no way I could *not* spend a few minutes discussing the changes

Jesus initiated during the Last Supper and about His introduction, through the Communion service, of the New Covenant. Then, with gratitude, all of us except Bess and Joe shared the matzo and wine of Communion. I concluded our Seder by praying for the peace of Jerusalem and for the Jewish people throughout the world. I also prayed that all our people everywhere would come to know personally our Passover Lamb.

The service ended with prayer in our Messiah's name.

We didn't leave the table until after nine P.M. I was relieved when Bess and Joe said they couldn't remember when they had enjoyed Passover more—"even if you did talk about Jesus."

The Question

The next morning the entire family, with the exception of Bess and Joe, sat together in church. We enjoyed a memorable time of worship, which included some moving messianic music. In my sermon I spoke about Passover, about the faithfulness of God in delivering our people from the judgment that fell on the firstborn in all the houses of Egypt, and about how God brought an end to Israel's bondage.

After the service was over, Jennifer turned to her mother, Judy.

"Mom," she asked, "why didn't Aunt Bess and Uncle Joe come to church today?"

"Well, Jennifer," Judy explained slowly, "Aunt Bess and Uncle Joe are Jewish, but as yet they don't believe in Jesus. That's why they weren't with us."

Jennifer thought for a moment. Then she persisted and asked the big question I've been leading up to: "But, Mom, how can you be Jewish and not believe in Jesus?"

The sheer logic of it stunned Judy, who shared the conversation with Ethel and me later. Out of the mouths of babes!

Remember What Jesus Said

Later, as I thought about Jennifer's question, I remembered a passage that had struck me when I was trying to prove that Jesus was not our Messiah. It was the first time I had ever read the Gospel of John. The context was where Jesus was speaking to some Jewish leaders:

> ". . . I know you. I know that you do not have the love of God in your hearts. I have come in my Father's name, and you do not accept me; but if someone else comes in his own name, you will accept him. How can you believe if you accept praise from one another, yet make no effort to obtain the praise that comes from the only God? But do not think I will accuse you before the Father. Your accuser is Moses, on whom your hopes are set. If you believed Moses, you would believe me, for he wrote about me."
>
> John 5:42–46

This statement convicted me. Why? Because I knew all about being Jewish, but I knew nothing about the Tenach, our Bible. I wasn't even sure I believed that the Bible is the Word of God. In fact, I wasn't even sure at the time that I believed in God.

And that is the truth each of us must grasp as we think about and pray for the Jewish people. While many of them know the major stories of the Bible, they do not know the messianic prophecies or understand who Moses was referring to when he said, "The LORD your God will raise up for you a prophet like me from among your own brothers. You must listen to him" (Deuteronomy 18:15).

As for Jesus, when He said, "If you believed Moses, you would believe me, for he wrote about me" (John 5:46), I think He was referring to more than Moses the man. I think He was referring to the entire Hebrew Bible—the Law, the prophets and the writings. All of it speaks of Jesus and reveals God's will for the Jewish people.

Proverbs 30 leaps to mind. I had never heard this important portion of Scripture discussed in the synagogue or anywhere else before I became a believer:

> "Who has gone up to heaven and come down? Who has gathered up the wind in the hollow of his hands? Who has wrapped up the waters in his cloak? Who has established all the ends of the earth? What is his name, and the name of his son? Tell me if you know!"
>
> verse 4

If I had really believed in the God of my fathers, and that the Bible is His Word to us, I would have studied it more carefully. I might have been able to see the provision He made so that we could be redeemed from the curses of Deuteronomy 28. Furthermore, I am sure I would have been able to join Jennifer in asking, "How can you be Jewish and not believe in Jesus?"

But then the scales were still on my eyes.

As you intercede for the Jewish people in general, and for the ones you know, pray that a mustard seed of faith will be planted in each of them. Pray that the scales will come off their eyes and that they will be able to see that they can remain Jewish and believe in Jesus. In fact, the most Jewish thing a Jewish person can do is to believe in Jesus!

But we must do more than pray for the Jewish people. We must reach them. How? That is what we will consider next.

How Do We Reach the Jewish People?

If Jesus returns tomorrow, then tomorrow I'll rest from my labor. But today I have work to do. I must continue the struggle until it's finished.

Dietrich Bonhoeffer

Have you ever gone to a Jewish funeral? If you have, you know that while the twenty-third psalm might be read and wonderful things said about the deceased, the rabbi does not seek to awaken any hope that there is life beyond the grave for Jewish people. Life is over, and there is nothing else. Over the centuries our rabbis have quoted the sages who, in *The Ethics of the Fathers*, said, "One hour in this world is better than an entire world to come." So Jewish funerals are very sad.

For most of my life I did not believe in heaven. I thought it was a Christian myth, something Catholics invented in order to scare their kids.

What do I believe about heaven now that I am a follower of Messiah Jesus? I believe—indeed, I know, as all Christians know—that heaven and eternal life await me. What awaits those who do not believe? Only judgment. They shall "die in [their] sins" (John 8:24).

Because of this dark prospect, David L. Larsen writes at the conclusion of his book *Jews, Gentiles and the Church* (Discovery House, 1995):

> A final duty is incumbent on believers everywhere. In the light of Christ's commands to live in constant readiness for His return and in view of the constellation of signs of the approaching end of the age, particularly in relation to Israel, we need a strong and growing sense of spiritual urgency in the mission and ministry our Lord has entrusted to us.
>
> p. 336

Larsen adds that Jesus' return "is imminent, and we must assist others in boarding the ark of safety before the deluge of judgment falls."

I don't know how you feel as you read these two statements. But I trust that in view of all you have read in Scripture and in this book so far, you have become increasingly convinced of the validity of Larsen's concern. Each of us needs a sense of urgency in the ministry to which God has called us; and with Jesus' return imminent, we have urgent work to do. One of the greatest joys any believer can experience comes from being used by God to lead others, especially Jewish people, to their Messiah and Savior.

In this chapter we will look at some effective ways we can do just that. But first, since it is exciting to learn the process by which others come to the Lord, let's glance at attempts that have been made historically to share the Gospel with Jewish people.

A Quick Two Hundred Years

For almost two centuries, Bible-believing Christians in many nations have sought to share their faith in Jesus with Jewish people. "The London Society for Promoting Christianity Amongst the Jews" was formed in 1809. This ministry, a society of the Anglican Church, later became known as "The Church's Ministry Among the Jews." Its members still keep busy throughout England, central Europe and Israel.

Another mission to the Jews in Europe, as the Reverend Bruce Lieske points out in his booklet *Witnessing to Jewish People* (Board of Evangelism Service of the Lutheran Church–Missouri Synod, 1984), was the Berlin Israel Mission. Founded in the early 1820s, it influenced Franz Julius Delitzsch (1818–1890), a Jewish believer, to form another mission to the Jews in Leipzig in 1869. In 1877, after many years of work, Delitzsch completed a translation of the New Testament into Hebrew.

Among Lutheran theologians of note were two Jewish scholars: Carl Paul Caspari (1814–1892) and August Wilhelm Neander (1789–1850). Neander, born of poor Jewish parents, was named Mendel at birth but took the name Neander ("new man") at his baptism in 1806.

The Norwegian Israel Mission was formed in 1844, the Finnish Missionary Society in 1859, the Swedish Israel Mission in 1875, and the Danish Israel Mission in 1885.

What success did these groups have in reaching Jewish people with the Gospel? Lieske quotes Forbert Blumstock (who cited as his source *The Jewish Encyclopedia*, 1916, Vol. IV) that in the nineteenth century, about 250,000 Jews in the British Isles and Germany became followers of Jesus. Most Jewish evangelism, according to this study, was accomplished not by the societies themselves but by members of local churches. These studies also show that long before there was a State of Israel, Bible-believing Christians felt deep concern for the salvation of the children of Israel.

Various methods were used by these agencies to spread the Gospel. Street evangelism was one key method. Its purpose: to facilitate face-to-face encounters with Jewish people who had no previous contact with the followers of Jesus. Bible portions and tracts were distributed. Discussion was encouraged.

Later other methods were used to bring unsaved friends, Jewish as well as Gentile, to informal evangelistic meetings. Additionally, relief was provided for immigrants, and job training as well as job placement.

Over the years efforts were made to reach larger groups more quickly via radio and later by television. God blessed these efforts, and as a result many Jewish people received Jesus as Lord.

Since 1967

We have acknowledged that the restoration of Jerusalem to Jewish authorities in 1967 is widely recognized among evangelicals as the fulfillment of biblical prophecy in our time. What does it mean for us? Nothing less than that it is now time for us, as God's ambassadors, to help bring the Gospel to the Jewish people.

This insight has led to a substantial increase in Jewish evangelism. And the growing number of Jewish people all over the world since 1967 who have confessed Jesus as Messiah and Lord reveals the blessings of God on these efforts.

How many Jewish people now believe? Since no records are kept by a single source, it is impossible to say. Some guess (as I have already pointed out) that there are between 80,000 and 100,000 Jews who believe in Jesus in the United States alone. Could the total be as high as 150,000 to 200,000 worldwide? No one knows for sure.

With the enlarged interest in reaching Jewish people, many are looking for more effective methods to reach them quickly. With evangelism, as with so many activities in American society, we want results *now.* We haven't become known as the microwave generation without reason! But manmade formulas are not always successful. Let me explain.

Gentile Christians are largely unaware of the difficulties many Jewish believers encounter in their search for a believing congregation in which they will feel at home. Even Jews who were non-observant prior to their belief in Messiah Jesus find it difficult to assimilate into the Gentile Christian world. Then there are the Jewish believers who avoid Gentile churches altogether because they do not feel at home in them. The problem is complicated further when they encounter occasional residual anti-Semitism in the Church.

Your eyebrows might have gone up at that last statement. Residual anti-Semitism in the Church? Like what?

In chapter 2 I told you how I felt when I heard a renowned Bible teacher use the term *Judaizers.* It wasn't his use of the word that bothered me; it was his tone of voice. I had heard the same tone in avowed anti-Semites when they said the word *Jews.*

So how do you think a Jewish person feels when he or she sees a Gentile—especially a Gentile Christian—roll his eyes at the mention of the Holocaust? Or talk about how he "Jewed that guy down" and got a better buy on some product or service? Or when he pokes fun at Jewish physical characteristics? Or when he declines to contradict a comment that Jews do this or that? Caricatures of any kind can hurt, and Jewish caricatures encountered in the Church hurt even more. Speaking of caricatures,

191

does anyone really believe that all Jews are wealthy? Or that the Jews control the government? Or the press?

"Telchin," you might say, "aren't Jewish people being too sensitive about these things?"

It's possible. But most Jewish people I know (and I'm sure we have this in common with many ethnic minorities) have highly tuned radar hidden in the hairs on the backs of their necks, and when those hairs start to stand up straight, they are most likely experiencing anti-Semitism. (In the next chapter we will look at ways Gentile believers can be more sensitive to Jewish people.)

Suffice it to say, given the relationship of the Church to the Jewish people over the centuries, and the difficulties many Jewish believers encounter in their search for a believing congregation, we cannot resort to quick-fix formulas in reaching Jewish people with the Gospel.

What Attracts Us to the Gospel?

One day when I was talking about this book with Bob Mendelsohn, former head of the Jews for Jesus office in Washington, D.C., I mentioned that I hoped to conduct a survey about what helped Jewish people make the decision to accept Jesus as Lord. Bob told me that a similar survey—one that asked what first attracted Jewish people to the Gospel—had been done in the early 1990s by Jews for Jesus.

At Bob's suggestion I contacted Jews for Jesus headquarters in San Francisco. They graciously agreed to let me send someone to their office to go through the survey responses. Then Bob told me about Chri Del Monte, a Jewish woman from Brazil who is a believer and a friend of his. Chri, who lives in San Francisco, was more than willing to help. The following week, after going through

1,187 out of 4,500 responses (taken at random and not otherwise screened), Chri called with the results.

Here is what those 1,187 replies revealed to the question, "While you were yet an unbeliever, what first attracted you to consider the Gospel?"

Response	Number	Percentage
Christian friends	332	28%
Jesus Christ/Holy Spirit/God	134	11%
A believing relative	113	10%
A life crisis	111	9%
Bible/Gospel	83	7%
A mixed marriage	53	4%
A vision/feeling/supernatural dream/miracle	39	3%
A pastor	39	3%
General search	36	3%
Friends who seemed at peace	21	2%
Messianic prophecies	17	1%
TV evangelists/radio shows	17	1%
Curiosity	17	1%
A book	16	1%
Jews for Jesus	16	1%
Billy Graham	12	1%
Old Testament study	11	1%
Searching for Jewish roots	10	1%
Miscellaneous other attractions (fewer than 10 each)	110	9%

There is no getting away from the observation that, in addition to the power of the Holy Spirit, the primary initial attraction came from believing friends and relatives. Something in their lives attracted the responders enough that they were willing to listen as the Gospel was presented. Notice the supplemental attraction—"friends who seemed at peace"—that drew these Jewish people to Jesus.

The two next-largest groups, "a life crisis" and "the Bible," are extremely important and should be considered together. A life crisis often causes us to call out for help that is beyond human solutions. Here is when we look upward and call out, "God, if You are there, please help me!" Here, too, is when many turn to the Scriptures for help, guidance and comfort—some for the first time.

Clearly no one event or experience first attracts all Jewish people to the Gospel. Understanding this fact helps us realize that we Jews are just like everybody else. Though we often resemble one another on the outside, we are very different on the inside. No one formula, method, ministry or technique attracts all Jews to the Gospel.

What Helps Us Decide to Accept Jesus?

A survey I took by mail in February 1996 of a thousand Jewish believers in the Mid-Atlantic states asked this question: "What was the one (or two) most important factor(s) in your coming to the Lord?" This is the survey question I told Bob Mendelsohn I wanted to ask. I wasn't looking for what first attracted a person to the Gospel as much as I was looking for the *principal* factor in their decision to accept Jesus as Messiah and Lord.

Almost seven percent of the people, or 68 of them—an excellent response, according to direct mail standards—gave 106 answers. In most cases more than one significant factor led them to receive the Lord. Here is what their answers revealed:

194

Response	Number	Percentage
Study of the Bible	42	39.6%
Testimony of believing friends	33	31.1%
Testimony of saved relatives	10	9.4%
Preaching of Gospel by minister	8	7.5%
Prayers of the saints	7	6.6%
Other	6	5.7%

The survey itself, though modest, reveals the truth that the Gospel itself "is the power of God unto salvation" (Romans 1:16, KJV). Most often the Gospel message is revealed to a person as he or she is reading the Bible. At other times it is revealed through the faithful testimony of God's witnesses.

Because I think you will enjoy them, I am including excerpts from some of the responses I received.

Reading the Bible

Bob, who has been a believer for 25 years, put it this way:

It was 1971. I was nineteen and looking for meaning and relevance. Jesus was the preeminent hippie!—that's what I read in the New Testament. Reading that Book is the number-one reason I am saved.

Lisa, who has been saved for four years, reported:

Reading the Bible was by far the most influential factor in my coming to the Lord. As I began to read, I found I had numerous misconceptions about what Judaism and Jewish history were all about. At first I felt completely lost and had many questions, which I wrote down in my journal. Gradually, as I read on, I began to grasp many basic

195

concepts, and my understanding deepened. The more I studied the Bible, the more I saw Jesus' life prophesied in the Old Testament. I read the Old and New Testaments over the course of a year.

After the first three months, I became convinced that Jesus was the Messiah, and as I continued in my studies, my conviction deepened. I know that my decision to come to the Lord was strictly between myself and God. I am certain that the foundation of my faith is rooted solidly in the Word of God and not in anything any human has told me. I knew I still had my doubts and fears and concerns, but I also knew I could trust God to show me the truth, as He had in the past.

Marilyn has been a believer for seven years:

When I turned thirty, my husband and I decided to start a family. At that time I began to think about which religion I would raise my child in. I was raised as a Conservative Jew and my husband was a non-practicing Presbyterian. I began to feel there was a God who cared about me, and I had a desire to search for a way to reach Him. I began to attend various churches, including a Unitarian church, sort of New Age cult, and just about every denomination. I even went to an astrologer and practiced meditation. I continued to feel emptiness and a longing to know God.

It wasn't until my sister-in-law, who is a born-again Christian, left a Bible at my house that I began to get the answers I so desperately needed. When I read the prophecies in the Old Testament and how they were fulfilled by Jesus Christ, I was totally amazed. A few days later I received Jesus as my personal Messiah and began my walk with the Lord.

I thank God every day for giving me the desire in my heart to know Him, and for my sister-in-law, who provided me with God's Word.

The Love of the Saints

Barb has been a believer for thirteen years. She wrote:

> The love that was shown to me, and that was evident about me in the churches I visited, provoked me to jealousy. I wanted what they had! I never found it in the synagogues I had attended and where I had been very active.

Scripture Plus Personal Assurances

Lorie, who has been saved for three and a half years, wrote me a long letter. (I'll refer to more of her comments in the next chapter.) She wrote, in part:

> Over nine years I studied Scripture on and off. And I began to think about my own mortality. Did I want to go to the grave thinking that a dark hole was all that awaited me? Fear ripped through me, and an equally strong thought raced around my head: I needed to believe in God.

Time continued to pass. Then one day,

> I passed by a local church and something inside me said, *Check this out.* I went in soon after. The pastor there, an exceptional expository preacher, led a congregation of warm, friendly, Bible-believing people. Then came the invitation. By this point I had grown to believe that Yeshua was most likely the Messiah, but I was having trouble accepting Him as the Son of God. I kept fearing that God would be so terribly angry at me for breaking the second commandment about not worshiping false gods. Suddenly I felt my feet moving. Too shocked at this event, I clung to the chair in front of me. No! I was a Jew and I was not going to walk down that aisle.
>
> An almost uncomfortable blast of adrenaline shot through me, but I clung tight and eventually left the building. But it made me think of the Scripture I had been hear-

ing or reading repeatedly over those previous weeks—the one that said that Yeshua would keep on knocking, but if we hardened our hearts too much, He would eventually leave us alone and we would never become part of the family of God. Terrified that this might happen, I invited the pastor over for a talk.

My main concern was for the pastor to reassure me that he would continue to view me as a Jewish believer. I did not view myself as a "convert" or as having changed faiths. I merely saw it as an enhancement of my own. He provided me with that assurance prior to leading me in the sinner's prayer.

The Preaching of an Anointed Minister

Mark has been a believer for six years. Here is how he answered my question:

> First I was struck by the realization that my way was not working anymore. No matter how hard I tried to make things right, my desperation grew deeper and deeper. I was invited to a church service and went in without any preconceived ideas. The Holy Spirit touched my heart and began working in my life.
>
> Second, once I decided to look into Christianity and try to figure out who or what Jesus is, the Lord made many Christians available to answer my many questions.
>
> The most important realization came to me that just because I am Jewish did not mean I could not follow the Lord.

Three Separate Factors

Sue has been a Jewish believer for sixteen years. She listed three factors that helped her come to faith:

> First, believers loving me and praying for my salvation. Second, reading both Testaments as one Book and find-

ing that the New Testament answers the prophetic questions raised in the Old Testament regarding the Messiah and other issues. And third, my own search for truth and meaning. I was hungry and thirsty and broken, and the Lord found and met my every need.

The Light Bulb Phenomenon

Mason has been a believer for only six months. He wrote:

> Two deciding factors "pushed me over the edge" to accepting Jesus as the Messiah. One was realizing that God does not operate the way I want Him to, and that in order to have a relationship with Him, it would have to be on His terms rather than my own. I also realized that there is always a price to forgiveness and that there can be no true forgiveness without one side bearing its cost.
>
> Initially the concept of sin was difficult to accept. I gradually began to see, however, that although I was not an evil person, there was still no means by which I could, through my own good works, be unconditionally right and acceptable with a perfect and holy God.

Three Ways We Must Be Faithful

These varied responses should confirm to us that different people are attracted to the Gospel in different ways. But in the final analysis, I say again, the Gospel itself "is the power of God unto salvation." The good news is that Messiah Jesus has given us access to God and made us fit for His friendship.

In a moment we will get to the question you picked up this book for—the question I've been leading up to all along: How do we reach Jewish people with the good news about Messiah Jesus? How do we communicate what we know is true to people committed to not hearing the truth? One of my wife's best friends told her once, "Even if it's true, I don't want to believe it."

The fact is, God has a way for us to reach the Jewish people that He provides in the book of Romans. But before we discuss it, I want to mention three things we need to be faithful in, in order to be effective in our witness.

1. Show Love

One thing is certain. Especially with Jewish people, love must be our motivation. God said to the Jewish people, "I have loved you with an everlasting love; I have drawn you with loving-kindness" (Jeremiah 31:3). I am certain God chose the words translated *everlasting love* and *loving-kindness* carefully. They are very important words. They reveal God's nature and character. God *is* love. And despite the transgressions of the Jewish people, His heart is filled with everlasting love and loving-kindness for them.

There is no way to get around the personal implications of this truth. If Jesus is Lord of our lives, we must be "love people." At home. With our parents. With our wives or husbands. With our teenagers. In school, with teachers and fellow students. At work, with our employers, employees and fellow workers. In church. Indeed, wherever we are, we must manifest the love of God for all to see. We must be signs of the Kingdom of God—signs of God's bright tomorrow in today's dark world.

This is not to say we are to be puppets or robots or laughing dolls out of touch with the reality of the world around us. Jesus sent us forth to be "wise as serpents, and harmless as doves" (Matthew 10:16, KJV). But again, the motivation behind our desire to bring the good news of Messiah Jesus to people who do not yet know Him, whether they are Jews or Gentiles, is love.

Our love level is to be so strong that when our friends, neighbors, fellow students, co-workers and all strangers detect it in us, they will know we are different and want to know why. Although frustration and disappointment may cause bitterness and even anger to rise up in the lives of our neighbors, the love of God in us and for us will help us rise above such reactions. Because we are believers, God makes it possible for us to walk in love in the midst of the most adverse circumstances. After all, that's what the Christian life is all about (see Romans 8:35–39).

I will never forget something that happened in 1982 when I led a tour to Israel. On the second day of our tour, we visited an *ulpan*, a school where non–Hebrew–speaking immigrants are given a crash course in Hebrew. The director of the school, whom I will call Dvora, spent more than an hour with the 29 people in our group explaining what it's like to teach Jewish immigrants from more than seventy nations to speak Hebrew.

When Dvora was finished with her excellent presentation, one of the non-Jewish members in our group got up and told her how much she appreciated the lecture and how much she loved the Jewish people.

Dvora smiled as she responded, "Don't tell me, show me!" Now that's something to think about.

2. Demonstrate Unity

In John 17:20–23 Jesus prayed for our unity. By our unity, He said, the world will know that He came from His Father.

But all too often down through her long history, the Church has demonstrated disunity to the world. And this disunity has concealed the identity of Jesus and prevented many from considering the life-transforming Gospel.

One of my favorite spiritual lessons is the story about the Tower of Babel found in Genesis 11. The people in Babel, as you remember, were in total agreement. They declared as one man that they would build a tower, a city and a name for themselves. Here is how God reacted to their agreement: "If as one people speaking the same language they have begun to do this, then nothing they plan to do will be impossible for them" (Genesis 11:6).

The place of agreement, God was saying, is the place of power. When people determine to work together in agreement to accomplish their goal, they can do anything, despite individual differences, that they can imagine.

To stop construction, God could have loosed a bolt of lightning. He could have opened the earth and swallowed up the men building the tower. But He didn't do either of these things. Instead He confounded the people's speech, making it impossible for them to understand one another. By doing this He broke their power of agreement, and before long the group was scattered all over the earth, never to be heard from again.

God does not want His children scattered all over the earth, never to be heard from again! At a time when the nations of the world are caught up with their individual agendas—a time when war and rumors of war fly all about us—God wants His people united.

Can you imagine how the Church will stand out when we are in total unity? Can you picture the power that will be released when we set aside our differences and agree with one another to do the will of God? Can anything we imagine to do be withheld from us? Even the gates of hell will not be able to withstand us (see Matthew 16:18)!

3. Obey Jesus

There is one more thing. If we love the Lord, we are to obey Him (see Luke 6:46; Matthew 7:21). We are to love the people He loves and carry His message of love to all the world—especially to the Jewish people, since the Gospel is "to the Jew first" (Romans 1:16, KJV). Jesus said, "If you love me, you will obey what I command" (John 14:15).

What were some of the things Jesus commanded? He was very specific:

> "All authority in heaven and on earth has been given to me. Therefore go and make disciples of all nations, baptizing them in the name of the Father and of the Son and of the Holy Spirit, and teaching them to obey everything I have commanded you."
>
> Matthew 28:18–20

Love. Unity. Obedience. That's what God wants to see in His Church.

With these truths firmly in mind, we are now ready to consider how God wants us to reach the Jewish people.

God's Way to Reach the Jewish People

The apostle Paul labored long and hard to present his missionary concerns to the Church. "Salvation is come unto the Gentiles," he explained in Romans 11:11 (KJV). Why has salvation come to the Gentiles? The reason is the key to reaching the Jewish people. Again in Paul's words: "To provoke them to jealousy."

God's way of reaching the Jews with the Gospel, then, is both specific and clearly perceived. Let's consider that key word *jealousy*.

My computer-generated concordance (*Enhanced Strong's Lexicon*, Woodside Bible Fellowship, 1992) tells me that the Greek word in Romans 11:11 for *to provoke to jealousy* is *parazeloo*, related to *zeloo*: "to zealously affect; to be zealous in the pursuit of; to exert one's self for; to be the object of the zeal of others; to be zealously sought after." Clearly this word calls for action. For what purpose? To make jealous the people toward whom we are directing our zeal.

But we have been taught that jealousy is an undesirable trait. What is the biblically acceptable sense of this word? Paul goes on to describe his hope that "I may provoke to emulation [again, *parazeloo*] them which are my flesh, and might save some of them" (verse 14, KJV). We are to be zealous in the pursuit of causing Jewish people to emulate us and our relationship with God, to have zeal for the One we have zeal for.

Note, too, that Paul was not recommending passivity in our relationship with Jewish people. Clearly He was recommending action.

Let me be very clear on the next point: Provoking someone to jealousy is not a matter of stressing the externals of our lives—where we live or where we go to church or how much money we have or how successful we are. Nor is our Jewishness (or non-Jewishness) the primary issue. Paul knew by the power of the Holy Spirit that only when the Jewish people are jealous enough of our relationship with God and with one another will they forget their fears and prior conditioning and long for what the followers of Jesus have.

How Do We Provoke Them to Jealousy?

This next question is related to the previous one: How are we to provoke the Jewish people to jealousy? Can the Church provoke jealousy by listing the accomplishments of her scientists or public servants or entertainers or musicians or journalists or writers? We would suffer by comparison.

How then are we, the Church of the living God, to provoke the Jewish people to jealousy? Here are just a few ways.

Peace

In the last chapter I mentioned the name of a dear friend of ours, Heidi, who attended our Passover Seder the year Jennifer asked that all-important question. But I didn't tell you anything about Heidi. I'd like to introduce you properly to her now.

Her real name is Heyde Carneiro Martins de Souza. She came to the United States from Recife, Brazil, in 1968. Despite her college education and prior work experience as a teacher, she could not obtain employment in her field. So, like many immigrants, she sought work as a housekeeper. It was our good fortune in 1969 to hire Heyde to work for us.

The first thing we asked her to do was let us call her "Heidi." We all laughed when she agreed to do so. Heidi worked for us more than nineteen years. During that time she became like a member of our family. To this day we are very close. But let's get to the story I want to share with you. It's Ethel's story, really:

"Soon after Judy became a believer," Ethel says, "while we were in the midst of trying to disprove the Messiahship of Jesus, Heidi and I used to sit in the kitchen over a cup of coffee reading the Bible. I would ask her all sorts of questions. Here I was, the mistress of the house—the woman who could go anywhere she wanted to go and do anything she wanted to do, having a cup of coffee with the woman who lived below stairs and waited on us hand and foot. But while I was upset about what my daughter had done and the danger this posed to our entire family, Heidi was loving and compassionate and understanding. I remember saying to her, 'Heidi, you've provoked me to jealousy!'"

That's actually the way Ethel put it.

A few months later, after Ethel became a believer, she was studying the book of Romans and came upon Paul's statement that "salvation is come unto the Gentiles, for to provoke [the Jews] to jealousy." When she read it she almost howled.

"That's what I said to Heidi!" she exclaimed.

Ethel explains her reaction this way: "Heidi had something I didn't have. I didn't know what it was then, but I learned later it's the peace that passes all understanding. Heidi also had this tremendous trust that God would see her through every trial. I had neither of these. And I was jealous."

Love

How else can we provoke the Jewish people to jealousy? The apostle Paul provides us with a clue. He wrote, with the wisdom from above, that the Messiah in us is our "hope of glory" (Colossians 1:27).

Do you remember the Greek proselytes who came to worship in Jerusalem and said to Philip, "Sir, we would like to see Jesus" (John 12:21)? In the same way, today's unbelieving Jews (and Gentiles!) would like to see Jesus. They look at us but want to see Him. They want to see the difference He has made in our lives.

We impress no one—and certainly fool no one!—by merely saying that Jesus is Lord of our lives. As a matter of fact, we should not even have to make this statement. People should know, by watching us and seeing the love level of our lives, that we are believers in Jesus (see John 13:35).

Even as I write these words, I sense the Holy Spirit convicting me of the ways in which I do not always manifest the love of God. I am sure you have experienced the same conviction.

Living the Gospel Here and Now

So, provoke Jewish people to jealousy through the peace that passes understanding and the love of Messiah Jesus. If you have been born again and have read the book of Revelation, you know what awaits us: heaven and eternal life. We are deeply persuaded of these realities because of our confidence in the promises contained in Scripture. Unbelievers, by contrast, have no such certainty.

But what about our lives right now, here on earth? How convinced are we that our God will never leave us nor forsake us? How firmly do we know that we are more than conquerors and overcomers in this life? Do we act on the truth that no problem or crisis can overtake us without God's permission? Do we know that all adversities can be overcome by His grace and power? Are we convinced that God is faithful? Are we certain that He will not let us be tempted beyond our ability to bear it?

Our daily lives must reveal to our friends—and everyone who sees us—the truth that only God makes it possible for us to withstand all that we do without losing our joy or blessed hope. In fact, it is our very confidence in Him, our love, our unity, our obedience and the victory we experience in our lives, that make us credible as we share our testimony with those who do not yet know Jesus. *We* are the message that our Jewish and non-Jewish friends, neighbors, classmates and co-workers first hear and must hear. And only when our *internal* message is right will they listen more readily to the *external* message we seek to share with them.

207

This does not mean we have to be perfect before we can share the Gospel with Jewish people (or with anyone else). It means we have to get back to God's priorities in our lives. Each of us can do this right now.

A friend of mine, Richard Harvey, who lives in London, is a missionary to the Jewish people. He is also president of the International Messianic Jewish Alliance. I e-mailed him asking what prescription he would write for someone who wants to help reach the Jewish people for the Lord. He e-mailed back this response:

> To witness to Jewish people, you don't have to be an expert or a trained missionary, but you do need love, boldness and sensitivity. The rest will follow.

A Special Word about Rejection

You know from all you have read so far that many Jews will not be willing to hear anything you have to say about Jesus. That's a given. But don't let their negative reactions keep you from doing what God commands you to do.

Further, be careful not to allow their rejection of the message to overwhelm you as the messenger. Remember, it is fear of rejection that keeps many Christians from sharing the Gospel with their Jewish friends. This fear is not from God. Recognize the source of it and take authority over it in the name of Jesus. Then, in obedience to His Great Commission, continue to do what He has asked you to do.

You are accountable for no one's behavior but your own. What does that tell you? That you are not responsible for how another person reacts to the Gospel. But you *are* accountable for your obedience in sharing the Gospel with all who have ears to hear. And this includes— no, it *starts* with—the Jewish people.

Bob Mendelsohn, former head of the Jews for Jesus office in Washington, D.C. (whom I mentioned earlier in this chapter), offers a suggestion to help us overcome our fear of rejection: "We should leave the Jewish people alone as much as Jesus did." Jesus didn't worry about rejection. Neither should we.

Over the years I have heard many people suggest how to witness to Jewish people. Many of these teachings center on the use or avoidance of certain words, and prescribe that we use language that facilitates communication rather than language that inhibits it. Like what? Like saying *believer* instead of *Christian*, *Messiah* instead of *Christ*, *congregation* instead of *church*, *tree* instead of *cross*. Most people find it difficult to hear words that threaten them, and Jewish people, as you know, often hear words like *Christian*, *Christ*, *church* and *cross* as threatening.

But there is much more to evangelism than using correct words.

I listened to a message Bob Mendelsohn gave in early 1996 at Fourth Presbyterian Church in Bethesda, Maryland. With his permission I summarize some of his points in this section.

Early in that message Bob stressed something we don't often think about. It comes from a story most of us are familiar with—the time Jesus asked the disciples who people were saying He was.

> They replied, "Some say John the Baptist; others say Elijah; and still others, Jeremiah or one of the prophets."
>
> Matthew 16:14

Then Jesus asked a more pointed question:

> "But what about you?" He asked. "Who do you say I am?"
>
> verse 15

209

We may not recognize that if Jesus had not asked the disciples that question, "Who do you say I am?", Peter might never have confessed Jesus to be "the Christ, the Son of the living God" (verse 16).

Here's Bob's point: Unless you get into somebody else's space and ask the pointed question, he or she may never confess Jesus as Messiah and Lord.

We like the words *friendship evangelism*. They have a comforting ring and assure us that we won't be rejected— because what kind of friend rejects a friend? We all need friends and should enjoy letting our lights shine before our friends.

But sooner or later we have to go beyond the "friendship" part and get to the "evangelism" part. We can't just sit around shining until someone asks us to tell him or her about Jesus. Jesus has sent us out not to wait until someone asks, but to preach. Sooner or later we have to ask our friend who Jesus is. And, as I have said, we must not focus on our fear of rejection. Let's focus, rather, on the fact that unless our friend confesses Jesus as Lord, he or she will be eternally separated from God! If you want to know what rejection is, that's the ultimate rejection.

So we must do all we can do to make certain that each and every one of our relatives and friends—and all who have ears to hear—never have to suffer that kind of rejection.

How to Initiate Conversations with Jewish People

Here are ten suggestions, taken from Bob Mendelsohn's message at Fourth Presbyterian Church, in simplified and paraphrased form, which offer Gentile believers in Jesus help in initiating conversations with Jewish people.

1. *Make the decision to witness to your Jewish friends.* We are not talking about witnessing to every person who walks down the street. We are talking about witnessing to the Jewish people who are already your friends.

2. *Determine whether or not your friend is Jewish.* There is a great deal of intermarriage today. Indeed, 52% of all Jewish marriages involve a spouse who is not Jewish. So having a Jewish name doesn't necessarily mean that person is Jewish. Think of Whoopee Goldberg. Further, many people who have at least one Jewish parent are not committed Jews. Knowing whether people are Jewish is important because it helps you determine how best to communicate with them.

3. *Ask sympathetic questions—questions you don't know the answers to.* Asking questions is a good way to involve people in conversation.

4. *Share a word of personal testimony.* A *word*, not *words*! Use a brief testimony. Make it quick. Keep it short. Tell your story in one minute. Help the Jewish person understand that all Gentiles are not automatically Christians. Why? Because most Jews think Christians become Christians the way Jews become Jews: They are born.

5. *Ask thought questions, opinion questions.* Engage the mind of the Jewish person. Show that you value his or her opinions. Many Jews (like me!) have been brought up with an us-them mentality—"us" Jews and "them" Christians. Show them you are not their enemy. Reveal your love for them. But never love people in order to get something from them! That's manipulation, prostitution. We are to love them be-

cause they are worthy of love. Jesus loved them enough to go to the cross to die for them, and He told us to preach to them in His name.

6. *Then* stop. *Stop talking.* These first six steps can be considered pre-evangelism steps. They are designed to break down the wall between Jews who cannot hear and you who are trying to communicate, and to create an atmosphere for further communication.

7. *Answer all questions from the Hebrew Bible—the Old Testament.* Your friend may not have one handy. You may have to use your own Bible to refer to the messianic prophecies.

8. *Get him or her involved in a regular Bible study.* This does not mean getting your friend to come to church every week. But it may mean getting him or her to a home group meeting or midweek Bible study. Find a safe place where Jewish people will feel comfortable enough to take their minds off themselves and their fears and consider the Word of God. Such meetings should not go on indefinitely, but for three to six weeks. They should also be organized in such a way that ongoing questions can be addressed.

9. *Ask for a decision.* Do what Jesus did when He asked the disciples, "Who do you say that I am?" The point is, after you have been discussing who Jesus is for several weeks, and after you have answered your friend's many questions, it is time for him or her to make a decision. Remember, you are not trying to get him to accept your point of view, but to recognize who Jesus is and to confess Him as Lord.

10. *Follow up.* This is where you take the person from where he or she is, with almost no knowledge of New Testament practices, and slowly walk him or her through the essentials of our faith. This takes

time. It involves discipleship. And it often makes the difference between whether or not the new believer grows to maturity.

My Postscript

I end this chapter with a powerful reminder:

Love is patient, love is kind. It does not envy, it does not boast, it is not proud. It is not rude, it is not self-seeking, it is not easily angered, it keeps no record of wrongs. Love does not delight in evil but rejoices with the truth. It always protects, always trusts, always hopes, always perseveres. Love never fails.

1 Corinthians 13:4–8a

God's way to reach the Jewish people is the way of love.

13

The Special Needs of Jewish Believers

Some months before I started working on this book, I received a telephone call from a pastor in the Midwest whom I will call Tom. He had read my book and was becoming acquainted with my ministry.

I could hear the enthusiasm in Tom's voice as he said, "Two Jewish people got saved in my church last Sunday night!"

Just as I was about to rejoice with him over this wonderful news, Tom added, "Tell me, Stan, what am I supposed to do with them?"

I was struck dumb by this question. After a moment of silence I blurted out, "Shoot them! They will never be closer to God."

Then it was Tom's turn to be stunned into silence.

A moment later I asked, "Tom, why did you ask that question? What do you think you're supposed to do with them?"

Long pause. Then Tom said, "That's why I called. I don't know many Jewish people and I don't know how to minister to them. Shouldn't I be sending them somewhere?"

There it is. That's the question. The impression among many non-Jewish believers is that Jewish people need to be "sent" somewhere. Why is that? Is it because the non-Jewish believer thinks the Jews know the Old Testament so well that it will be hard to teach them anything? Or is it because the non-Jewish believer doesn't know many Jewish people and is intimidated by the fact that a person is Jewish?

After my initial shock at Tom's question, and his shock at my response, we got into a serious discussion of how a pastor is supposed to minister to any new believers. He is to treat them as newborn babies. He is to love them, care for them, teach them the Word of God, guide them as they adjust to the reality of being new creations in the Lord, and see that they are discipled. It's best if he can be the discipler, but if he cannot, he should make sure another mature believer accepts this responsibility.

How Much Does Cultural Identity Matter?

I want to use the question Pastor Tom asked as an occasion to say something about the church I pastored for fourteen years, and about cultural identity.

The Living Word Fellowship had an interesting congregation mix. At one point ten percent of our members were Jewish, forty percent came from Catholic backgrounds and the other fifty percent from what seemed like every branch of Protestantism.

Every race was represented. We had Indians from India as well as American Indians, Hispanics from several countries, Korean and Chinese members and many African-Americans. It was as if God had scooped up all the people

He had selected for our congregation and dropped them into our midst. I won't say there were never any strained interpersonal relationships during those years. But I am proud of the fact that we managed to set aside the things that ordinarily divide us as we concentrated on the One who unites us.

Despite many problems, I found pastoring the Living Word Fellowship a glorious experience. It helped me recognize the beauty of cultural distinctives and (apart from language barriers) encourage their expression. At the same time, in the Church I see many cultures becoming one as we lay aside our differences and become "one new man" (Ephesians 2:15) who is "neither Jew nor Greek" (Galatians 3:28).

This does not mean God will someday eliminate all cultural distinctives. One of the last words in the Bible tells us God will dwell with those who are His "peoples"—the literal meaning of Revelation 21:3. So diversity gives us a foretaste of heaven. But I do not believe God will reserve separate sections in heaven for Baptists, Lutherans, Episcopalians, Presbyterians or any other denomination; or for Jewish believers apart from ones who are black, brown, yellow, red or white.

I share these things with you to increase your comfort level in working with Jewish people. But my opinion must not determine your views. We must look to the Word of God for guidance about how people from different backgrounds are to live together as brothers and sisters in the Lord.

Many people get caught up in examining the "trees" contained in Paul's epistle to the Romans—specific issues like justification by faith, righteousness, the faithfulness of God, sin and Israel—and tend to lose sight of the "forest," Paul's purpose in writing this magnificent book. As an apostle and missionary, he longed to share the Gospel with Jews as well as Gentiles. But he also wrote this letter, I believe, because of strains and divisions that had arisen between messianic Jews and messianic Gentiles.

Paul wanted to encourage them to put aside their differences and experience the unity God longs for in His Church. So in this epistle he stressed the individual themes I just mentioned in order to illustrate the truth that both Jewish and Gentile believers are in the same position. They face the same issues and underlying problems, and cannot rely on their ethnic identities as Jews or Gentiles to deliver them from these problems.

Certainly that theme is evident in Paul's statement in Romans 10:12: "There is no difference between Jew and Gentile—the same Lord is Lord of all and richly blesses all who call on him."

And listen to Paul's plea, following a discussion of the new peace between Jew and Gentile, in the first few verses of Ephesians 4:

> As a prisoner for the Lord, then, I urge you to live a life worthy of the calling you have received. Be completely humble and gentle; be patient, bearing with one another in love. Make every effort to keep the unity of the Spirit through the bond of peace. There is one body and one Spirit—just as you were called to one hope when you were called—one Lord, one faith, one baptism; one God and Father of all, who is over all and through all and in all.
>
> verses 1–6

We must never put our desire to honor any cultural identity ahead of our desire to please God who is, in the words of Ephesians 4, "over all and through all and in all." In everything in our lives, Jesus must be preeminent (see Colossians 1:18).

A New Movement

Still, I want to remind you of what many Jewish people fear: "If we accept Jesus, we will no longer be Jews." And recall the reaction of many of us when we see a cross. The cross reminds us of the terrible things done to us in the name of Christ over the centuries—the Crusades, the Inquisition, the pogroms.

Then there is the concept originating with some of the early Church Fathers that God is through with the Jewish people, that all the blessings He promised Israel now belong to the Church. Over the centuries this point of view has been repeated and developed so that now it has become a "theology." Sometimes it is called replacement theology or supersessionism, which is how Walter Riggins refers to it in his book *The Covenant with the Jews: What's So Unique About the Jewish People?* (Monarch Publications, 1992):

> [In] the Church's doctrine of 'Supersessionism'—the Church has superseded Israel as the chosen people of God. In other words, some Christians teach that the Church has replaced Israel altogether in God's love and purposes, leaving no place at all for Israel, which is rejected by God.
>
> p. 51

Obviously few Jews would be comfortable in a church espousing this point of view.

To try to ease Jewish fears, a new movement has emerged in the last twenty-plus years. I am referring to messianic congregations within the movement called messianic Judaism.

By adopting synagogue forms—wearing *yarmulkes* (head coverings), *tallithim* (prayer shawls), reciting He-

219

brew prayers, displaying a Torah (the first five books of Moses in scroll form), calling their spiritual leader *rabbi*, celebrating the Jewish feasts, and meeting on Friday nights and Saturday mornings—proponents of messianic Judaism hope to alleviate the fears of many Jewish people about the possible loss of their Jewishness. By exalting Yeshua within the context of synagogue life and emphasizing His Jewishness, they seek to promote an alternate way of preaching the Gospel to Jewish people. The synagogue environment, they feel, lessens the fear many Jews have of words like *Christ* and *cross* and *church* and *Christian*.

Reactions

Many non-believing Jews see the techniques of messianic Judaism as manipulation, entrapment and trickery. Many believing Jews as well as Gentiles see them as unscriptural. They have no problem with the concept of "messianic congregations" made up of Jews and Gentiles worshiping the Lord together, but they react strongly against the concept of messianic "Judaism." We must be very careful about this, they advise. As Jewish and Gentile believers, we have a New Covenant with God not tied to any form of rabbinic Judaism.

It must also be pointed out that being Jewish is an internal reality. No amount of externals can make one Jewish and no lack of externals can take one's Jewishness away. Further, synagogue life occupies only a small part of the attention of most Jews in America today. Our greater concerns are for the survival of the Jewish people and the State of Israel, caring for Jewish youth and the elderly, and supporting Jewish charities—indeed, standing behind all Jewish priorities. Also, Jews all over the world have become acculturated within their nations more than they have to a specific form of liturgical practice. As a result, most Jews today are secular. Further, when most new Jewish believers see the words *Christ, cross, church* and *Christian* from God's perspective, they overcome their fear of them.

It is beyond the purpose of this book to evaluate messianic Judaism. Suffice it to say, it has strong and vocal adherents, even as it has strong and vocal opponents, among both Jewish and Gentile believers.

Have messianic Judaism and messianic congregations erased the fears of Jewish believers and proven the best way to reach Jewish people for the Messiah? In terms of numerical results, one would have to observe that, whereas some congregations have grown, others have not. One would also have to observe that in North America, the vast majority of people attending messianic services are not Jewish. Also, most of the Jewish people who have come to faith in recent years attribute their decisions (as we saw in the last chapter) to the faithful and loving witness of Gentile Christians.

But this does not mean the total number of messianic congregations is diminishing. Today there are four separate associations within the movement, ranging from evangelical to charismatic. And in North America there are approximately 130 congregations. They all seek to create an environment in which a Jewish person will feel more comfortable.

"Am I the Only One?"

Do you remember in the last chapter, when we were considering the responses to the survey I conducted, that I mentioned Lorie and told you she wrote me a long letter? Lorie admits she is not typical of Jewish people who accept Jesus as Lord. But her letter addresses some of the very issues we have been discussing. I think you will benefit from reading in more detail what Lorie has to say.

She explains that she found a messianic congregation eighty miles from her home and began to attend services on Saturday mornings.

While there, I don't have to worry about well-meaning Gentile believers trying to mold me into something I was never meant to be. I don't have to stare at crosses, which have always made me uncomfortable. I don't have to worry about being treated as though I'm somehow different. I don't have to hear pastors stating erroneously that the entire nation of the Jews murdered Christ (and believe me, I hear it said that way). No one there calls Judaism "a false, satanic, apostate religion" or defines it as a religion built on ethics.

While I understand these statements and definitions viewed through a particular theological perspective, I still find them offensive, especially when they come from Bible-believing, Bible-reading Christians. Had I heard these statements from my own pastor before I joined his church, I would never have joined.

Do I still attend my old church? Faithfully. Every Sunday morning I go to services with my husband and children. But now I have the strength to stand up and say, "Trying to 'Gentilize' me is just as wrong as Judaizing was wrong in Bible days."

Do I still have my times of doubt and fear? Of course! I constantly battle feelings of animosity toward Church leaders who revere rampant anti-Jews like Justin Martyr, Constantine and even Martin Luther. I struggle with the problem that the modern Church has largely continued to rob our faith of its Jewishness, even when most pastors know Church history fairly well.

Worse still, I battle the realization that modern doctrine is tainted because of early attempts to eradicate its Jewish roots. But through it all God keeps reminding me that He loves me and has directed my life. I am where

222

He wants me to be, and when doubts arise I cling to Him, pray for steadfastness, forgiveness and a renewal of trust.

Here's Where *You* Come In

Lorie gives us a lot to think about, doesn't she? In light of her experiences, you can surely understand many of the problems she had with the Church. Probably others are harder to grasp. But if you reflect thoughtfully on the feelings and fears she expressed, you can understand why a messianic congregation played an important role in her spiritual development.

How grateful to God I am that all over the world, on-fire children of the living God within the Church have come to recognize the mistakes of the past and are working together to overcome them! More changes must still be made, of course. But I am confident they *will* be made as the Church sees God at work among the Jewish people.

I have pointed out that the needs of every person are distinct. But we can draw some general principles from Lorie's experience that will help every believer be more sensitive to the needs of Jewish people. Let me suggest the following:

1. Don't try to use any formulas. Meet the person where he or she is and build from there.
2. Recognize the lack of knowledge that most Jewish people have about God, the Old Covenant, the New Covenant and Jesus.
3. Understand their deeply ingrained fear that if they accept Jesus, they will no longer be Jews. Counteract this fear from Scripture. Reinforce their identity as Jews.
4. Pray for the Jewish people you know.
5. See each person as an individual.

6. Let God's love motivate you in all you say to him or her.
7. Don't be in a rush to get him or her to make a decision to accept the Lord. Recognize there will be many questions, and use these questions as opportunities to look to Scripture for the answers.
8. Remember what our survey showed—that most Jewish people accept the Lord because of what they discover in Scripture. Also of critical importance: the love and testimony of believing friends and relatives.

Some Special Needs of the Jewish Believer

We have come a long way together in this study. Now it is time to begin applying what we have learned—not just to our minds, but also to our hearts, and to our conduct toward the Jewish people.

I probably don't have to stress again that God longs to redeem Jewish people from the curses of Deuteronomy 28 and give them eternal life (see John 3:16; 17:2–3; 2 Peter 3:9). Also, if Jesus is *not* the Messiah and Redeemer of the Jewish people, He is not the Lord and Redeemer of Gentile Christians either.

But knowing what the will of God is and knowing how to do God's will are two different things. Whether you are a pastor, church leader or just an "ordinary" member of the church, I'd like to help you be more effective in reaching out to and receiving Jewish people.

First, try to understand the pressures many Jewish people face when they first become believers. Many, like Lorie, require reassurance that they are still Jewish. They need to internalize the truth that, even as Jesus was Jewish in His humanity, they, too, will always remain the physical descendants of Abraham, Isaac and Jacob. Also, many of the Jewish people you lead to the Lord will suffer rejection from significant people in their lives—family as well as friends.

Especially during the early months of the new believer's walk, your fellowship and affirmation are very important.

My own experience is a case in point. I told you in chapter 1 about the reaction of my friend Shirley to the news that I had become a believer. To her, my act of faith meant I was no longer Jewish. Some Jewish people had even stronger reactions. Old friends refused to have anything more to do with me. Colleagues with whom I had worked for a long time suddenly told me they could no longer do business with me. One neighbor actually spit in my wife's face one day when Ethel greeted her on the street. One of my relatives didn't speak to me for more than ten years. Another spit in my face when we met at an uncle's funeral.

I'm not saying another person's experience will be like mine. Much has happened within the Jewish community since July 3, 1975, when I was born again. Since then more and more Jewish men and women have come to the Lord, even in Israel, and the reactions of other Jews worldwide have become much milder.

Even so, help your Jewish friends who come to the Lord prepare emotionally for the negative family and social reactions they may experience, and be ready to comfort them when this occurs. It always helps to remember the words of Jesus to Jews who did not yet know who He was:

"I have come to turn 'a man against his father, a daughter against her mother, a daughter-in-law against her mother-in-law—a man's enemies will be the members of his own household.' Anyone who loves his father or mother more than me is not worthy of me; anyone who loves his son or daughter more than me is not worthy of me."

Matthew 10:35–37

This is not a prescription for action by a new Jewish believer against those in his family who are having difficulty accepting his decision! But the lesson is clear: New Jewish believers must remember that, before He laid the foundation of the earth, our omniscient God knew the reactions of family members and friends to their decision to follow Jesus. It is important that they learn the truth of 1 Corinthians 10:13:

> There hath no temptation taken you but such as is common to man: but God is faithful, who will not suffer you to be tempted above that ye are able; but will with the temptation also make a way to escape, that ye may be able to bear it.
>
> (KJV)

God will always provide us with the strength to remain faithful to Him.

Try to help new believers grasp that an entirely new life has been opened to them. They need to be taught what it means to be a new creation in Messiah Jesus. With Him at the center of their lives, "old things are passed away; behold, all things are become new" (2 Corinthians 5:17, KJV).

A Word for Pastors

How does a local pastor communicate these truths to a new believer? As a loving father helps his own children. A pastor needs to be affirming and reassuring. He or she should help these new believers build relationships with others in the congregation, Gentiles as well as Jews, and introduce them to people who have a heart for Jewish people, so they become integrated into the community of faith.

Whether it takes a few weeks, a few months or even longer, the pastor should maintain contact with them and be available to answer their many questions. If his congregational activities are too demanding for this sort of personalized attention, he should encourage a member of his staff, or people from within the congregation, to help provide this nurturing.

There is no greater work a pastor can do than transform the members of his congregation into genuine disciples of Jesus and equip them to disciple others (see Matthew 28:19).

I will never forget how important it was for me to find that there were people available to help and encourage me in the early months of my own walk with the Lord. Because of my hunger to be discipled, I determined after I became a pastor to become a disciple-maker myself. So each year for many years, I selected six or seven men to disciple, and spent twelve to eighteen months meeting with them at least twice each month.

Seeing them grow was a thrill! And after they were discipled, they helped to disciple others. Our congregation tried to follow the admonition given in 2 Timothy 2:2: "The things you have heard me say in the presence of many witnesses entrust to reliable men who will also be qualified to teach others."

Every new believer needs assurance of his salvation. He or she also needs to understand how to pray, study Scripture, lead a holy life, witness, participate in godly fellowship, handle temptation and be used by God in ministry.

What a tragedy that so few pastors have the time or inclination to provide discipleship training in their congregations! I must emphasize this: As important as discipleship is for a new Gentile believer, it is even more important for a new Jewish believer, who probably has no understanding of the attributes of God, or the different kinds of prayer, or how to study the Bible. And the subject of holiness can be a real eye-opener! The same with knowing how to apply God's Word to the circumstances of life. It often takes much teaching on these subjects, as well as faith to believe God's way works, before we see results in a person's life.

May I add a final admonition? It offends Jewish people to be singled out publicly in our congregations for no other reason than that they are Jewish. In many churches Jewish believers are treated as mascots and "show-Jews." Throughout history we Jews have sought to be accepted as individuals, not just because we are Jewish. This holds particularly true when we become believers.

Let your public celebration of the fact that Jews are coming to the Lord be a celebration only of His faithfulness.

Advice from People in Ministry

I put a question to four of my friends active in Jewish evangelism worldwide: "If a believer contacted you and asked how he could be more effective in reaching Jewish people for the Lord, what would you tell him?"

1. Build Relationships

Helge Aarflot, general secretary of the Norwegian Church's Ministry to Israel in Oslo, Norway, points out that building relationships is the first step.

> Without relationships, all our methods are wasted time and money. Our methods can be as good as possible but will seldom work in the long run. With solid relationships

the methods can be poor, but one doesn't have to worry. You can be direct, even rude, and you will not scare the person.

So build relationships first! Personal relationships in different roles and capacities constitute the most important precondition for any effective outreach. The challenge is not how to tell, but how to be listened to; not the preaching of the Gospel, but the reception of the Gospel.

2. Jews Need Jesus!

Moishe Rosen, former executive director of Jews for Jesus in San Francisco, has five answers to the question of how to be more effective reaching Jewish people.

The first thing the Church needs to know is that there is no way of salvation apart from Jesus. Obviously if we Jews could have it our way, we would find some other way. We would want to make it less difficult for our beloved family members and Jewish friends to receive their salvation. But either we take the Word of God, as expressed in John 14:6 and Romans 9–10, on this critical point, or we will be carried about by various winds of doctrine through wishful thinking.

Jews need Jesus to be saved. And if Jesus is not for Jews, who is He for? It almost seems a waste of energy for Him to have been born in Bethlehem and then tell Nicodemus he had to be born again (John 3:3), if Jews don't need to be born again.

The second thing Rosen points out is the tendency of many Christians to do "good" instead of "right."

It is right to be friendly. It is right to be humble. It is right to be loving. It is right to be helpful. It is right to feed the hungry. But unless it is our purpose and intention to witness to every single person as soon as possible, with the

229

knowledge that the Lord might come at any moment and that ours will be the last witness, then we do an injustice to these people.

The idea that you can take time to build friendships is a denial of the imminent return of our Savior. Nowhere in Scripture does it say we are to win people to ourselves. We are to win them to the Lord.

Third, Rosen provides a special word to pastors:

The pastors' role in witnessing is crucial. While most pastors are so busy ministering to Christians that they have little time to be with non-Christians, it is essential that they take the lead in getting out and seeking the lost themselves. If they want the members of their flock to do something, they must show the way. It is not enough to exhort people to do something. You must exemplify what you want done.

A significant fourth point Rosen makes is this:

There are no real experts on witnessing to Jews. Each Jew and each Gentile is unique in himself or herself and presents a unique set of problems and challenges to the person doing the witnessing. It is far better to take people as you find them, and take them as you go, than it is to come up with formulas. The Church needs to know there are many Jewish people looking for God. They need to know the Holy Spirit has not retired, nor has God decided not to do anything until a specific ministry, formula or method is created.

Finally Rosen observes that we spend too much time emphasizing the difficulties rather than blessings of reaching out to Jewish people:

It is the most significant thing we can do. If you sow enough Gospel seed, you will reap a great harvest.

3. Be Equipped

John Ross and Mike Moore of Christian Witness to Israel in Kent, England, sent their advice by fax:

> To be more effective in witnessing to Jewish people, we would urge the pastor to mobilize his church membership for the task. Jewish people need to be included in the outreach programs of the local fellowship, and particularly with churches situated in the midst of Jewish communities. Indeed, all churches should retain an adequate supply of suitable evangelistic literature. Most Jewish people come to the Lord through the witness of "ordinary" Christians rather than through mission agencies.
>
> Christians need to feel as confident about witnessing to Jewish people as they do to anyone else. By stripping away the mystique that often surrounds the Jewish community, a pastor can help his congregation understand that although Jewish people are different from everyone else, in another sense they are the same as everyone else. Their understanding of God and His Word are as flawed as that of Gentiles, and their religion and covenantal standing before God will avail them nothing in the last day.
>
> [Gentile] Christians need to be equipped, however, to evangelize their Jewish friends and neighbors in a manner sensitive to the Jewish psyche and culture. Pastors should enlist the aid of organizations that have experience and expertise in working among the Jewish community. Seminars to heighten an awareness of Jewish history and give practical instruction about how—and how not—to witness to Jews are essential for any organization that takes seriously the spiritual needs of the Jewish people.

4. You Will Be Blessed

Sam Nadler, executive director of Chosen People Ministries in Charlotte, North Carolina, was going out of town when my question reached his office. So he asked Larry Rich, manager of the office in North York, Ontario, to respond. Larry faxed me an outline highlighting many of the biblical reasons for reaching out to the Jewish people. We have covered most of these. But he emphasized a point Rosen also touched on, one I have not stressed enough.

I want to join them both now in reinforcing the truth of Genesis 12:3: "I will bless those who bless you, and whoever curses you I will curse; and all peoples on earth will be blessed through you."

Meditate on this verse! Do you really believe you will bless Jewish people by leading them to the Lord? If you don't, reread chapter 10. If you do, know that God will bless you because you are blessing them.

Reaching Out from the Church

It refreshed me to read some comments recently from Roy Schwarcz, congregational leader of "Lights of Israel," part-time pastor of evangelism for Chicago's Moody Church and a Jewish believer who has been involved with several messianic congregations. Writing in the May 1996 issue of *The Lausanne Consultation on Jewish Evangelism Bulletin*, in an article entitled "Jewish Outreach through Your Local Church," Schwarcz observes:

> We need the church. This may sound over-simplistic yet for many years and indeed to the present day many of us continue to act as if we do not need the church. Dare we admit to ourselves that a great impetus for starting the Messianic Congregational movement was because of anger and frustration toward the church? Anger because of its failure to recognize the Gospel's Jewish connection. Frustration grew from the fact that when we pointed this failure out

to the church, we were accused of building a wall of partition—when in fact they had built the wall. . . . For many years I was frustrated with the failure of the local church to be actively involved in Jewish ministry.

p. 17

But today, after years of service with messianic congregations, Schwarcz sees greater opportunities available—"opportunities that may escape us should we remain complacent and inwardly focused."

For two reasons our mandate should now be to bring our acknowledged Messianic identity into the church. First it is God's vision for the church—Jews and Gentiles worshiping as one in the Body of the Messiah. And second, because the church is the greatest vehicle for winning Jewish people to the Messiah.

pp. 18–19

Schwarcz suggests four steps Jewish believers should take within the Church:

First, join a solid church whose membership is in daily contact with Jewish people. Second, educate the congregation that you have joined. This includes making yourself available to teach Sunday School, lead Seders, and work with the children's programs. Third, worship regularly with this church. Fourth, serve the church in whatever ways are needed, as a regular member of the congregation.

p. 19

If the Church is to provoke the Jewish people to jealousy, Schwarcz cautions that we must understand the Jewish roots of our faith. "When Gentile Christians experience the Gospel's Jewish connection," he explains,

233

"they will feel a kinship with the Jewish people that will blossom into a powerful witness."

Where Do We Go from Here?

Now that we have considered some of the special needs of Jewish believers and received advice from some involved in Jewish ministry, let's consider in our final chapter what the Church needs to do to reach out to and receive Jewish people.

14

What Does the Church Need to Do?

Let me begin this final chapter by making an observation about love. If you love someone, you must do something about it! I have never met a man who truly loved a woman who did not continually look for ways to express his love. He shows it in his eyes. He declares it with his mouth. He reveals it by his actions.

Do you remember the story in chapter 12 about Dvora, the *ulpan* leader in Israel? When the woman in our tour group started to tell her how much she loved the Jewish people, Dvora just smiled and said, "Don't tell me, show me!"

So it is important that you show the love of God—and your own love—to the Jewish people you know.

What if you don't know any Jewish people? How can you show love to people you don't know? The most important thing you can do is pray. Pray for the peace of

Jerusalem, certainly, but also for Jewish people wherever they are in the world.

One of Ethel's favorite stories involves Heidi, our former housekeeper, whom you met first in chapter 11 at our Passover Seder.

Go back with me in time to April 1976. Ethel had been saved for almost a full year. As summer approached, Heidi began to make plans for her vacation. That year she was going back to Recife, Brazil, and asked jokingly one day if Ethel would like to return to Recife that July. (Ethel had visited once before with our younger daughter, Ann.)

Ann, who was in college now, had obtained a scholarship to study art and would be away for most of the summer. So Ethel thought going to Recife with Heidi for a couple of weeks was a wonderful opportunity.

"And I'll be able to share my testimony at your church," Ethel offered.

That did it for her. She was going!

The reunion with Heidi's family in Recife was joyous. And the Sunday after they arrived in Recife, Ethel testified in Heidi's church, with the help of the pastor as interpreter. She recounted how it was that our entire family had received Jesus as Lord within a four-month period the prior year.

The people seemed particularly responsive to this testimony. They laughed in the right places. They wept with joy. They gave Ethel a standing ovation when she finished, and then came to hug and greet her.

Afterward Ethel found out why they were so responsive. The pastor explained to her, in front of the congregation, that Heidi had written him soon after starting work for us in the States, asking if the church would begin to pray for the salvation of the entire Telchin family.

So they had been praying for us for more than ten years, and they were thrilled to see this answer to their prayers.

Prayer works! As James 5:16 says, "The effectual fervent prayer of a righteous man availeth much" (KJV).

Pray and Share

So the very first thing the Church must do is pray for the Jewish people. Pray that God will grant them a mustard seed of faith. Pray He will send laborers to bring His Word to them. And pray they will have ears to hear.

After praying for the Jewish people in general, pray for them specifically. A friend of mine, a Jewish believer, told me he likes to stump his Gentile-Christian friends by asking, "What kind of Jewish person do you think is easiest to lead to the Lord?"

They usually respond by saying, "Secular Jews," or "Reform Jews."

"No," he responds with a smile. "The easiest Jewish person to lead to the Lord is the Jewish person you know!"

Which leads me to my next point. If you know any Jewish people, begin to pray for them by name. Pray that God will give you favor with them. Pray that He will anoint you to live the Gospel before them and give you an opportunity to share it with them.

The second thing the Church needs to do is put feet to her prayers. We have established in the last several chapters that there is no one way to share the Gospel with Jewish people. Yet God's way always works—and God's way is the way of love.

Once you have established relationships with people and let them know you care about them, it is easier to speak about spiritual matters. As Helge Aarflot stressed in the last chapter, by having good relationships with people, you help to ensure that they will hear what you have to say—even if they're Jewish.

When Pastors Are Jewish

I've told you about the church I pastored for fourteen years. You can understand why Jewish people felt safe and comfortable in that congregation. But I suspect they would feel safe in any church pastored by a Jewish person who loves the Jewish people.

Lon Solomon, for example. Pastor Solomon pastors McLean Bible Church in McLean, Virginia. He explained on the phone that while the church does not have a specific Jewish outreach, there is a large Jewish community in their area in suburban Washington, D.C., and word gets around about his being a Jewish pastor. Thus, McLean Bible Church has many Jewish members.

> Ours is a seeker-friendly church, and we take a seeker-friendly approach to ministry. We encourage people to bring their friends to church and take tapes of my sermons to their Jewish friends. Sometimes their friends express shock at hearing about a Jewish pastor. So our members encourage them to listen to the tapes.
>
> Every time we go out to reach people, we reach Jewish people. They are looking for spiritual meaning in life, and many of them are concerned about what will happen to them after they die. They find no real assurance of immortality in Judaism.
>
> We take a long-term view of evangelism, especially Jewish evangelism. We try to provide a safe place where people can process the information they receive until they are able to make their decision. One Jewish man came to church for three years before he made his decision. I have found that people aren't able to make snap

salvation decisions anymore. If we can get them to come regularly and listen, they will probably come to faith.

One other thing I should point out. We work very closely with the local branch of Jews for Jesus. Whenever we learn of a Jewish person who has come to church or expressed an interest, we let the people at J. for J. know, and they do the follow-up. It works out very well.

When Pastors Are Not Jewish

What about pastors who are not Jewish? What do they do to attract Jewish people to their churches, and how do they minister to them?

I contacted several pastors in different denominations, in different parts of the country, who have large numbers of Jewish people in their churches. I will highlight two of these in particular, and let the leadership of those churches explain their approach.

Create an Atmosphere of Acceptance

The Church On The Way in Van Nuys, California, pastored by Jack Hayford, has an especially large number of Jewish members. They keep no records on the ethnic or cultural makeup of the congregation, but they estimate the number of Jewish believers in their church as probably greater than 250 but fewer than a thousand.

What does Church On The Way do to attract and minister to Jewish people? Senior associate pastor Dan Hicks responded this way:

It is true that there are numbers of Jewish believers who attend Church On The Way, but it is important for you to understand why and why not. Due to the size of the Jewish population in our immediate region, it stands to rea-

239

son that we have an impact, because of the life of Jesus in many of our congregation who work side by side with Jewish people every day.

Additionally, it would be helpful for you to know that we have resisted the temptation to focus on any single ethnic group above another. Our stance has been, and remains, one of embracing anyone Jesus brings to us, and reaching out to all.

Among the various outreach ministries, however, we do have a specific group that meets and prays for the Jewish community in our area. Through this group, frequent contacts are made with Jewish people.

Some weeks later I spoke with Dr. Jack Hamilton, the former president of L.I.F.E. Bible College West and now senior associate pastor of Church On The Way. An important emphasis, he explained, is that people do not have to abandon their culture or heritage in order to become members.

We try to create an atmosphere of acceptance, rather than pressure the person to become "Christianized." We have a loving and caring congregation in which people feel safe. The atmosphere is not threatening or judgmental, but accepting.

At L.I.F.E. Bible College we didn't stress the study of Greek and only the incidental study of Hebrew. We *emphasized* Hebrew, so that our students would understand the roots of their faith.

Then there is Pastor Hayford's primal commitment to Israel, and his belief that one of the major signs that revival is coming has to do with what's going on among Jewish believers in Israel today. Pastor Hayford has been to Israel many times and has led tours to Israel.

I also know Pastor Hayford has addressed messianic Jewish leaders in Israel at least twice.

Intentionally Include Jewish People

When I wrote to Pastor Charles Schmitt of Immanuel's Church in Silver Spring, Maryland, I asked what they did to attract the fairly large number of Jewish people they have in their congregation:

> We have a desire to see Jewish people feel at home in our church. This desire springs out of a twofold vision from the Lord.
>
> First of all, we sense there is great prophetic significance in the Lord's redeeming work among Jewish people at the end of this age. We see from Romans 11 that God intends to visit His people Israel in a profound way in the last days—redeeming them, restoring them and engrafting them again into His holy purposes. "And so all Israel will be saved" (Romans 11:26) is an awesome and staggering end-time promise, and we as a church want to participate in that great happening! So we have begun to ask the Lord to make us a "Jewish-friendly" church.
>
> Secondly, we sense that the Lord has called His Church to be a multi-ethnic, multi-racial, multi-cultural body. We are called to be His "coat of many colors." He has broken down every ethnic wall by His cross and has washed away every racial separation in His precious blood (Ephesians 2:11–22). He now calls us to be one body, and that includes Jews and Gentiles of all sorts being joined together practically as "one new man" in the Church.
>
> I know this might be controversial, but I personally believe that God's highest purpose is not achieved in having separate black churches and Hispanic churches and Korean churches and Chinese churches and messianic synagogues in a given locality. I personally believe that our Lord's highest purpose is achieved in having local churches that are, in themselves, multi-ethnic, multi-racial and cross-cultural.
>
> When we fully accepted this vision as His will for us as a church, and intentionally gave ourselves to see this

241

happen, it did! We have become a beautiful, multi-racial, multi-cultural, multi-ethnic expression of the Body of Christ in our area.

Pastor Schmitt writes about how he includes Jewish people intentionally in his ministry:

My wife, Dotty, and I love to teach not only from the New Testament, but from the Old Testament, for that is the rich root and firm foundation of our faith in Jesus Christ. We have found that Jewish people love to hear the Old Testament taught with relevance.

Our worship, too, is drawn from the psalms of King David, replete with singing and Davidic dancing and instruments and banners. Our colorful Davidic banners contain many words and symbols from the Hebrew Old Testament.

Because we are a "celebration church," we are also into God's holidays, and we seek to celebrate as many of these as we can. As a Christian congregation, we celebrate the incarnation of our Lord Jesus Christ during the whole month of December. And Passion Week—with special Palm Sunday, Maundy Thursday, Good Friday and Resurrection Sunday celebrations—is a highlight in our spiritual year as we focus on our Lord's atoning death and glorious resurrection.

But we also celebrate the holidays the Lord gave Israel. They have become for us a powerful experience of spiritual "show and tell." We love to see Jesus, the Lamb of God, in the Passover. We delight to see the outpoured Spirit of Christ in the feast of Pentecost. We are stirred to see Jesus, the coming King, in the great fall feasts of Israel. Our sovereign God becomes alive to us in the book of Esther at Purim, and God's holy freedom-fighters are a stirring end-time challenge to us from the prophecies of Daniel in our celebration of Chanukah.

Our pilgrimages to Israel and public display of the flag of Israel as a touchstone for intercession for the "peace

242

of Jerusalem" also contribute to the feeling among Jewish people that we are part of their lives, and they are part of ours.

In these ways we believe we have become a Jewish-sensitive congregation, even as in other relevant ways we have intentionally sought to include African-Americans, Hispanics, Asians and people from other backgrounds into our experience of church life. I sense in all of this that we are experiencing a powerful foretaste of what heaven itself will be like, when we are all gathered around the throne of God "from every tribe and language and people and nation" (Revelation 5:9).

What Your Church Can Do

There you have it. Churches located three thousand miles apart share the same vision of the nature and function of the Church in today's world. But what can *your* church do to reach the Jewish people in your area?

It may be that not many Jewish people live in your community. In addition, you may not belong to a mega-church. In the United States, 85% of all churches have fewer than one hundred members. On the other hand, you may belong to a growing church with two hundred or three hundred or even five hundred members.

The location and size of your church are of little consequence. It is the heart of your church that matters.

You already know there are no quick formulas or easy ways to share the Gospel with someone. You also know we cannot save anyone. All we can do is share the Good News with those who have ears to hear.

Having said this, I want to provide a checklist of nine general suggestions and eleven specific suggestions to help you reach the Jewish people in your community. Underlying all twenty suggestions is this truth: God wants you to "enlarge the place of your tent" (Isaiah 54:2). He wants you and your congregation to pray for, reach out to and receive Jewish people.

General Suggestions

1. Agree that reaching the Jewish people is the will of God for these closing days of the Church before the Lord returns.
2. Pray specifically for the Jewish people.
3. Endeavor to make your church open, hospitable and attractive to Jewish people. Consider displaying a large menorah, the seven-branched candlestick patterned after the lampstand in the Holy of Holies of Moses' Tabernacle in the wilderness and in Solomon's Temple. The menorah is a familiar and comforting symbol to Jewish people. Even more important is the attention the pastor and leadership of the congregation give to the unique holidays and memorial days—Passover, Pentecost, Rosh Hashanah, Yom Kippur, Sukkot (Tabernacles), Chanukah, Purim—that God said the Jewish people were to celebrate forever, and from which the Church can learn much about the faithfulness of God.
4. Truly desire that Jewish people become members of your church.
5. Teach the great truths of the Old Covenant.
6. Visit Israel and messianic congregations there.
7. Be committed to multi-ethnic, multi-racial, multi-cultural churches.
8. Provide literature on Jewish culture and evangelism.
9 Be realistic. The entire Church cannot be sensitized to adjust to every believer and minority group. Accordingly, help new Jewish believers un-

derstand that there may be people in your church with no experience sharing their lives with Jewish people. Encourage them to be patient with these new friends. It is probably not anti-Semitism that new Jewish believers experience in your church, but lack of knowledge of the Jewish people. It is a lot easier to prepare the new believer for the church than it is to prepare the church for the new believer.

Specific Suggestions

1. Pray for, send money to and support Jewish evangelists.
2. Invite Jewish ministries to hold meetings in your church.
3. Use messianic music in your worship services.
4. Provide teaching about Jewish holidays as they occur during the year.
5. Hold special "Israel Night" activities (perhaps including The Day of Remembrance for the Holocaust Dead) or prayer meetings for Jewish people and invite your Jewish friends to these services.
6. Invite Jewish people to your home group meetings. Let them experience what God has done in your lives. And be prepared in this non-threatening environment to share the Gospel with them.
7. Conduct short-term Bible classes (three to six sessions) for Jewish inquirers.
8. Send volunteers to work with Jewish missions in Israel or New York or London or wherever you can connect with them. When they return, they will report on what God is doing among the Jewish people, and your church will never be the same.

9. Approach witnessing systematically. Develop a list of Jewish people to pray for, determine the best ways to reach them, and then do it!
10. Have your church members send greetings to their Jewish friends, especially during the Jewish holidays.
11. Invite Jewish believers to share their testimonies with your church. Encourage your members to invite their friends to these meetings.

First Things First

When I started to write this book, two thoughts came to my mind. First, I remembered that in all major life decisions, change begins in the heart. Second, I recalled that it is out of the fullness of the heart that the mouth speaks (see Matthew 12:34). That's why I prayed that God would help me reach your heart as well as your mind as you read this book. I trust that has happened. I trust, too, that you understand you must now act on what you know.

But where should you begin? Beginning with prayer always comes first. Ask God to give you the wisdom you need at this moment in your life. Thank Him for touching your heart with His love for the Jewish people and ask Him to guide you moment by moment as you now prepare to speak to them. Ask Him to show you where to begin and with whom. And then begin, depending on Him to give you the anointing you need with each individual. Ask Him, too, to help you share what you have learned from Scripture and this book with others so that they, too, will begin to pray for and reach out to their Jewish friends.

What is God's will for the Jewish people? He doesn't want any to perish, but all to receive eternal life (see

246

2 Peter 3:9). What is God's will for the Church? That she make His will her will.

I end this book now with a prayer: May God's grace, peace and anointing be upon you as you reach out to the Jewish people with His love.

Amen.

Now that you've finished reading this book, I'd love to hear from you. Here's how to reach me:

Stan Telchin Ministries
6210 N. Lockwood Ridge Rd., #143
Sarasota, FL 34243-2529
Phone: 941-907-3838
Fax: 941-907-9898
E-mail: stan@telchin.com
www.telchin.com

A Personal Note

What? No retirement?

So why does a man in his seventies start a new ministry?

That's a question I have often asked myself. After all, this is the time I should be enjoying the fruits of a lifetime of work. Right? I should be relaxing. Ethel and I should be planning vacation trips. I should be out on the golf course. After all, isn't that what people my age are supposed to do?

If I had never become a believer and had remained in the business world, I probably would have retired long ago and been leading "the good life." But I did become a believer and left the business world to enter the ministry, and my entire life changed.

I certainly do not have the money I would have had at this time in my life. But what I do have, money can't buy.

When God first called me into the ministry, He never talked to me about a retirement plan. Instead He kept showing me how I could be "refired" by the power of His Holy Spirit! He revealed to me the things He wanted me to do right then and there. But He also let me know He might be changing my instructions from time to time as I was ready for increased responsibility.

I loved being a pastor. People came to the Lord, were loved, cared for, taught the Word of God, strengthened

251

in their faith, set free, had their marriages healed, were discipled and equipped to do the work of the ministry.

But then the new assignment came and Stan Telchin Ministries, Inc., was formed. Here's our mission statement:

> To bring the good news of Jesus "to the Jew first, but also to the Gentile." We will achieve this goal by writing and publishing books and articles, appearing on radio and television programs, conducting seminars, providing teaching tapes, ministering to churches, leading trips to Israel and providing personal ministry in the United States and overseas.

As you can see, God has birthed a renewed desire in me to write, travel, teach and preach. He wants me to help call attention to what He is doing around the world, especially among the Jewish people. In the States I have ministered from New York to California, from Wisconsin to Florida. I have also ministered in Germany, England, Ukraine, Russia and Israel. Invitations continue to come in and dates are being worked out.

Wherever I go, I point to the fact that Jewish people all over the world are receiving the Lord. This hasn't happened solely because of a human movement or a method or even a messenger. It has happened by the power of the Holy Spirit breathing life into dead bones.

But many in the Church don't understand what to do about this phenomenon. That's why I wrote this book.

On a personal note I can tell you that Ethel and I are well. We have been blessed not only with wonderful children, Judy and Ann, but with four outstanding grandchildren: Jennifer, Zachary, Elizabeth and Nicolas.

I keep talking about getting back to playing golf again, and Ethel and I hope the schedule will ease up a bit so we can do some personal travel. But the call of God continues to resonate in my spirit and the telephone keeps ringing.

Ethel joins me in praying God's anointing on you as you take what you have learned from this book and share it with others. The time is growing short.

Maranatha!

Appendix 1

What's Happening in Israel?

One of the men in Israel with whom God has knit my heart is Baruch Maoz, a Jewish believer who has served the Lord for more than thirty years. Presently he pastors the Grace and Truth Congregation in Rishon Le Tsion, Israel. He is also director of HaGefen Publishing Company (the company that published *Betrayed!* in both Hebrew and Russian).

In order to obtain an update on what is going on today among Jewish believers in Israel, I contacted Brother Maoz, who e-mailed the following information:

> The most important statement that can be made on this topic is that there actually are Israeli Jewish-Christian churches in Israel today. No more than a decade ago, few in Israel knew of the existence of a community of Jews who believed in Jesus. Today their existence is common knowledge. Content for many years to live on the bare fringes of Israeli society and reach only the fringes with the Gospel, Jewish Christians are now found in the Army, in business and industry, and among the trained professionals.
>
> There is a flurry of activity among the Jewish Christians: two publishing houses, two very busy conference centers, a National Evangelistic Committee that organizes three to four outreaches every year, three magazines, a

pro-life movement, a drug-abusers rehabilitation center, a national intercongregational conference and two Bible colleges (one already functioning and the other soon to be). A wind of change is blowing in Israel.

The second most important statement that can be made about the Hebrew-speaking congregations in Israel today is that they are growing numerically. Every year or so another congregation comes into being. Some disappear overnight like mushrooms, but most continue to worship and witness. The number of Jewish Christians and their families is growing almost by the day.

You may have noticed, incidentally, that Brother Maoz uses the term *Jewish Christian*, while throughout this book I have used the term *messianic Jew*. Why is this? The answer is simple. In Hebrew the words *Yehudi Meshuchi* can be translated either *messianic Jews* or *Jewish Christians*. There is no distinction between the two terms.

How Many Jewish Believers in Israel?

As of March 18, 1996, the approximate number of messianic Jews with their families now living in Israel is more than six thousand. There are approximately 55 Hebrew-speaking congregations, 23 Russian-speaking and seven Ethiopian-speaking congregations to serve them.

To his e-mail letter, Maoz attached three articles that are called Jewish-Christian Occasional Papers (JCOP) or Jewish-Christian Occasional Articles (JCOA). Because the information in these papers and articles is so important, you should know what they contain.

In JCOP 54, Maoz points out that evangelism is legal in Israel. (What is illegal is giving gifts to induce someone to change his or her religion.) So various congregation members distribute tracts, place them in mailboxes, do newspaper advertising and hold special events to which they invite non-believing Jews. Also, the National Evangelistic Committee that Maoz mentioned conducts special drives in which believers from different parts of the country come and work together to share the good news of Yeshua with all who have ears to hear.

When I was in Israel in June 1994, I met a young man named Avi Mizrachi who had just returned to Jerusalem from a campaign in Haifa. He was thrilled with the results of that campaign and shared many of his experiences with me.

Although these campaigns are effective in rounding up the names of those interested in hearing more about Jesus, the primary and most effective form of evangelism in Israel is the same as it is throughout the world: one-on-one contact.

Growth in the number of messianic Jews in Israel is not limited to evangelism. Second-generation believers are becoming a reality. Immigration, too, especially from the former Soviet Union, is bringing many additional Jewish believers into the land.

Some Confusion Exists

Because of the newness of spiritual rebirth in Israel, some confusion exists among the various groups. Part of this confusion is understandable: How do these Jewish-Christian congregations relate to the broader body of believers and still retain their Jewish identities? (This problem is by no means unique to the United States.)

At present, each of the congregations considers itself independent with no obligation to any of the other congregations. Two of them, I understand, have chosen to follow a synagogical form. The others have not.

Because of the anti-Semitism of the past, many have difficulty relating to the wider Body of Christ. Many prefer no visible association with churches outside Israel, in order to maintain their Jewishness. They seek to develop a distinctly Jewish, though not rabbinic, form of worshiping the Lord. And in this, as one would expect, they are having some difficulty.

The Bottom Line

Brother Maoz writes:

Jewish-Christian congregations aspire to the salvation of our people. We share the apostolic conviction that Jesus is Israel's promised Messiah, the only means for our people's personal and national salvation. For that reason we long to be equipped by the Almighty for the important evangelistic task in which we are involved.

One senses, from reading the papers Maoz authored and forwarded, a longing in our brothers and sisters in Israel for a unity that will not destroy the individuality of distinct congregations but will reflect their oneness in the Messiah.

At the same time, these papers speak of many unique problems the Israeli believers are experiencing. Are they obligated to keep the ancient feasts of Israel? Are these cultural or religious obligations? How should they be kept (if indeed they are to be kept)? What about the relationship between Jewish and Gentile Christians? And Arab Christians?

Presently there are two seminaries in Israel and efforts are under way to start a third.

Difficulties Remain

The Church is viewed with respectful antagonism by the secular Israeli society (eighty percent of the people). The Orthodox view the Church with active disdain, and most cannot distinguish between Catholics and Greek Orthodox, between Copts and Protestants, between evangelicals and charismatics.

When Israelis see the often-bitter rivalries between these groups, they wonder where the love is that Jesus was supposed to have brought to His followers.

Many Israeli believers are still harassed. The more prominent ones have their phones tapped. Some experience trouble getting their mail. Some Jewish-Christian congregations experience vandalism. Often they are unable to rent facilities in which to hold their meetings. And although the majority of Israelis would probably not rise up to harm individual messianic Jews, few would probably come to their aid should trouble arise.

It is clear that as more and more Jewish men and women become followers of Messiah Yeshua, a national confrontation is brewing. Those who claim the Messiah has come are being confronted by those who insist He has not. The results of this confrontation will be far-reaching.

With what ultimate result? Remember the apostle Paul's statement that this would be "life from the dead" (Romans 11:15).

What the Church Can Do

The greatest need for the congregations in Israel is encouragement and spiritual support.

1. It is important to remember our Israeli brothers and
   sisters in prayer.

2. Visits from those who come to Israel is a tremendous encouragement, as are correspondence and financial aid.
3. Should overt discrimination against the Israeli congregations emerge, they would welcome an outpouring of requests to our own government to protest such discrimination.
4. Share the work by carrying the Gospel to Jewish people who live where you are.

Writes Brother Maoz:

Criticize us as brethren when we err. Do not support us or our country uncritically. It takes a friend to criticize and a true friend to listen. Please don't leave us in the hands of our mistakes, or of those of our unbelieving brethren.

JCOP 28

If you want to reach the Reverend Maoz for more information, contact him at P.O. Box 75, 75100 Rishon Le Tsion, Israel.

Appendix 2

Denominational Judaism in America

Several Jewish denominations emerged in America as a reaction to synagogue life in the ghettos of Europe. It was inevitable, when the immigrants left the ghettos and experienced life in the United States, that spiritual and cultural changes would take place. In the process three major denominations of Judaism came into being: Orthodox, Reform and Conservative. I will list briefly the highlights of each.

At the same time, I must point out that there is no fixed or absolute uniformity within each of these denominations. Some congregations in each denomination seek to be more Orthodox in their practices, others more Reform. I will also describe briefly the Reconstructionist movement and Humanistic Judaism.

It is important to recognize the difference between Judaism as it is practiced in Israel and the varied forms of American Judaism. Since a discussion of these differences is beyond the purpose of this book, I refer you for more information to *Two Worlds of Judaism* by Charles S. Leibman and Steven M. Cohen (Yale University Press, 1990).

Orthodox Judaism

Orthodox Judaism accepts the Hebrew Scriptures as the inspired, inerrant Word of God and seeks to uphold the unchanging faith of Israel. It is based on a legal system that establishes specific and precise Jewish behavior for almost every life situation. It recognizes the 613 commandments of God set forth in Scripture, but in practice emphasizes only some of them.

Among the chief Orthodox priorities is keeping the Sabbath from sundown on Friday evening until sundown on Saturday evening. Keeping the Sabbath includes not riding in automobiles or public conveyances during this period, as well as observing all the Talmudic provisions concerning what may or may not be done on the Sabbath.

Other priorities include avoiding all non-kosher foods, maintaining kosher kitchens (with separate dishes and utensils for meat dishes and dairy dishes), separating men from women in the synagogue and keeping heads covered at all times. Men wear skullcaps (called *yarmulkes* in Yiddish) or hats. Women often wear wigs called *sheitels*. Prayer in Hebrew is conducted three times a day—morning, afternoon and evening. School-age children receive religious instruction daily in the school attached to the synagogue or attend Hebrew school after public school each day.

The approximate number of Orthodox synagogues in the U.S. is 1,200 with a total membership of 1,000,000. (This statistic and those that follow are taken from *The World Almanac and Book of Facts, 1995*, copyright © 1994 by Funk and Wagnalls Corporation.)

Before we consider the other main denominations in Jewish life, a brief mention should be made of the *Chasidim*, the Hasidic Jews about whom Chaim Potok and others have written. (Because the *ch* sound in Hebrew is difficult for many to pronounce, the spelling is often given as *Hasidim*. The same pronunciation difficulty explains why the Hebrew word *Chanukah* often appears in English as *Hanukkah*.)

After World War II many survivors of the Holocaust came to America. Some were extremely Orthodox—indeed, ultra-Orthodox. Whereas the majority became more and more involved in and accepted as part of American culture, the Chasidim remained aloof. They were concerned primarily about retaining their form of Judaism. Although living in America, they formed ghetto-like pockets in which to segregate themselves, primarily in Brooklyn but elsewhere as well. (Indeed, many thousands of Chasidim live in different parts of the world.)

Almost as a caricature, Chasidic men can be identified by their beards, long black overcoats and black hats. Though there are many groups within Chasidism, the two primary movements are the Lubavitcher and Satmarer. Each group is led by its own charismatic rabbi and most have little to do even with other branches of Orthodox Judaism.

Reform Judaism

Reform Judaism has its roots in the eighteenth-century Enlightenment movement in Germany, which elevated rationalism over all traditional social, religious and political ideas. The Reform movement of Judaism in the United States began to take shape as early as 1824. By about 1870 it had become a significant denomination within Jewish life. It sees its primary task as adjusting Jewish theology to the accepted scientific and progressive theories of the day.

In 1875 Hebrew Union College was founded in Cincinnati under the leadership of Rabbi Isaac Mayer Wise. In America, Dr. Wise believed (according to Stuart E. Rosenberg in *The New Jewish Identity in America*, Hippocrene Books, 1985), Jews should produce their own unique expression of Judaism

> committed to moderate reforms, in the spirit of the age and place. Its intention was to maintain only such ceremonies as elevate and sanctify our lives, but reject all such as are not adapted to the views and habits of modern civilization.

> pp. 162–163

As practiced in the United States, Reform Judaism does not consider Scripture either inspired or inerrant divine revelation. Only the moral laws of the Bible are binding. The Reform Jew does not feel he must abide by traditional Jewish customs and practices that he feels are incompatible with modern culture and civilization.

The Sabbath is considered a time of personal rest and meditation without emphasis on keeping the Talmudic prohibitions. Religious services are held in a temple rather than a synagogue. In English-speaking countries, most Reform services are conducted in English. In other nations, the local language is used. Men and women are considered equal within the temple and may sit together. Women may be ordained as rabbis.

There are approximately 848 Reform temples in the U.S. with a total membership of 1,300,000.

Conservative Judaism

Conservative Judaism first appeared in the United States in the 1840s as a reaction to Reform Judaism. It emphasizes, according to Rosenberg in *The New Jewish Identity in America*,

> the norms and ways of Jewish life . . . a general avoidance of novel theological commitments. . . . [It is] uniquely the product of America and its particular history . . . [and] stresses Jewish tradition, even while it remains flexible in theological matters.

p. 172

The largest number of observant Jews in the United States are affiliated with Conservative synagogues. They see Reform Judaism as too liberal and too far removed from Jewish tradition, and Orthodox Judaism as too restrictive and incompatible with today's society.

Rabbi Joseph Telushkin in his book *Jewish Literacy* (William Morrow, 1991) describes the Conservative branch of Judaism:

> Conservative Judaism strikes a middle road between Reform and Orthodox Judaism. Unlike Reform, it considers itself bound by almost all Torah rituals as well as Torah ethics; unlike Orthodoxy, it considers itself free to introduce innovations in Jewish law, particularly in the laws formulated in the Talmud.

p. 97

Conservative Judaism does not stress keeping the Sabbath or observing *kashrut* (keeping kosher) as rigidly as Orthodox Judaism. Men and women may sit together in the synagogue services. Both Hebrew and English are used in the Sabbath, holiday and daily liturgies. Women may be ordained as rabbis.

The approximate number of Conservative synagogues in the U.S. is 800 with a total membership of 2,000,000.

Other Movements

Reconstructionism within American Jewish life was founded in 1922. It rejects belief in an all-knowing God who made a covenant with the Jewish people. It does not accept the Bible as the inspired Word of God. It believes that cultural bonds are more important to Judaism than religious doctrines. It holds that the survival of the Jewish people depends on their unity regardless of their religious beliefs and practices. It supports the State of Israel as the cradle of Jewish civilization and the focal point of Jewish people throughout the world.

There are approximately 60,000 members in the United States.

Humanistic Judaism came into being as a religious movement in 1963 in Detroit under the leadership of Rabbi Sherwin T. Wine. He formed the Society for Humanistic Judaism, which affiliated with the International Federation of Secular Humanistic Jews.

Walter Hellman, the leader of Humanistic Jews of Portland (Oregon), has explained on the World Wide Web:

> As Jews we take tremendous pride in the values developed by our people through the ages. These values include, among others, justice, love of family and learning, compassion and social responsibility. We want to maintain our connection to this heritage. We celebrate it by observing Jewish holidays and traditions and learning our history.
>
> Humanistic Judaism will allow Judaism to survive and flourish for ourselves, our children and the many other Jews who are unable to believe in supernatural authority for the guidance of human affairs.

Sherwin T. Wine in his book *Judaism Beyond God* (KTAV Publishing House, 1995) states that Humanistic Jews are eager to affirm that "Jewish history is a testimony to the absence of God and the necessity of human self-esteem."

Some Additional Information

Here are some interesting statistics about synagogue life in America, taken from David L. Larsen's *Jews, Gentiles and the Church* (Discovery House, 1995). Of the 5,750,000 Jews in the United States,

only 10% attend synagogue on a given Sabbath;
70% attend only four times a year;
40% are Conservative;
30% are Reform;
11% are Orthodox.

About 30% of the Jews in this country are married to Gentiles. In 1985 52% of marriages involving Jews were interfaith. Twelve percent of American Jews attend Christian churches.

Appendix 3

Agencies That Minister to Jewish People

It has been reported that within the United States alone are more than two hundred agencies concerned with Jewish evangelism. Listed below, in state order, are the names and addresses of some of the major agencies.

Arizona

Jewish Voice Broadcasts, Inc.
P.O. Box 6
Phoenix, AZ 85001
(602) 971-8502

Rock of Ages
8844 W. Daley
Peoria, AZ 85345
(214) 289-0965

California

Ariel Ministries
P.O. Box 3723
Tustin, CA 92681
(714) 259-4800

Fellowship of Messianic Congregations
P.O. Box 5628
Sherman Oaks, CA 91413
(818) 788-6702

Jews for Jesus
60 Haight St.
San Francisco, CA 94102
(415) 864-2600

Rock of Israel
P.O. Box 9200
Van Nuys, CA 91409
(818) 988-7131

Colorado

Christian and Missionary
Alliance
P.O. Box 35000
Colorado Springs, CO 80935
(719) 599-5699

Union of Messianic Jewish
Congregations
8556 Warren Ave.
Denver, CO 80231

District of Columbia

Jews for Jesus
P.O. Box 5594
Washington, D.C. 20016
(202) 362-1312

Florida

Jews for Jesus
240 N. Andrews Ave.
Fort Lauderdale, FL 33301
(305) 764-6365

Love Song to the Messiah
4751 N.W. 24 Ct.
Fort Lauderdale, FL 33313
(305) 733-0656

Menorah Ministries
P.O. Box 669
Palm Harbor, FL 34682
(813) 726-1472

Georgia

Sid Roth Ministries
Messianic Vision
P.O. Box 1918
Brunswick, GA 31521
(912) 265-2500

Illinois

American Messianic Fellowship
P.O. Box 5470
Lansing, IL 60438
(708) 418-0020

International Ministry to Israel
3323 North Ridge Ave.
Arlington Heights, IL 60004
(708) 394-4405

Jews for Jesus
P.O. Box 182
Skokie, IL 60076
(708) 679-2680

Maryland

Lederer Messianic Ministries
6204 Park Heights Ave.
Baltimore, MD 21215
(410) 358-6471

Messianic Jewish Movement
Intl.
P.O. Box 30313
Bethesda, MD 20824
(301) 656-7575

Ministry of Hope
P.O. Box 1388
Pasadena, MD 21122
(410) 360-0822

Song of Israel
57 Carona Ct.
Silver Spring, MD 20905
(301) 989-1328

Massachusetts

International Messianic
Jewish Alliance
P.O. Box 438
Hingham, MA 02043

Michigan

Messianic Outreach
of Grand Rapids
P.O. Box 3654
Grand Rapids, MI 49501
(616) 459-0778

Minnesota

Good News for Israel
P.O. Box 23018
Richfield, MN 55423
(612) 881-2311

Midwest Hebrew Ministries
4600 W. 77 St., Ste 227
Minneapolis, MN 55435
(612) 831-0284

Missouri

Assemblies of God
Division of Home Missions
1445 Boonville Ave.
Springfield, MO 65802
(417) 862-2781

Task Force on
Jewish Evangelism
Lutheran Church–Missouri
Synod
1333 S. Kirkwood Rd.
St. Louis, MO 63122
(314) 965-9917

New Jersey

Friends of Israel Gospel
Ministry, Inc.
P.O. Box 908
Bellmawr, NJ 08099
(609) 853-5590

New York

Camp Shoshana
(Ariel Ministries)
R.R. 1, Box 356
Keesville, NY 12944
(518) 834-6057

Chosen People Ministries
88 Southern Pkwy
Plainview, NY 11803
(516) 939-2277

Jews for Jesus
109 E. 31 St.
New York, NY 10016
(212) 683-7077

North Carolina

Chosen People Ministries, Inc.
1300 Cross Beam Dr.
Charlotte, NC 28217
(704) 357-9000

Oregon

Youth With A Mission
P.O. Box 4213
Salem, OR 97302
(503) 363-1571

Pennsylvania

Committee on the Christian
Approach to the Jews
1907 Chestnut St.
Philadelphia, PA 19103
(215) 568-1030

Eastern Mennonite Board
of Missions and Charities
P.O. Box 628
Salunga, PA 17538
(717) 898-2251

Messianic Hebrew
Christian Fellowship, Inc.
3232 N. 2nd St.
Harrisburg, PA 17110
(717) 238-6255

Messianic Jewish Alliance
of America
P.O. Box 177
Wynnwood, PA 19095
(800) 225-MJAA

Texas

The Christian Jew Foundation
611 Broadway
San Antonio, TX 78215
(512) 226-0421

Jews for Jesus
P.O. Box 802086
Dallas, TX 75380
(214) 783-2400

Rock of Israel
P.O. Box 270558
Dallas, TX 75227
(214) 289-0965

Zola Levitt Ministries, Inc.
13140 Coit Rd., Ste 318
Dallas, TX 75240
(214) 690-1874

Virginia

Chosen People Ministries, Inc.
819 Woodward Rd.
Marshall, VA 22115
(540) 364-1103

CMJ/USA
10114 Lawyers Rd.
Vienna, VA 22181
(703) 281-3751

YWAM Israel
Coordinating Office
P.O. Box 7736
Richmond, VA 23231-0236
(804) 230-8898

Bibliography

Coudenhove-Kalergi, Count Heinrich. *Anti-Semitism throughout the Ages.* Westport, Conn.: Greenwood Press, 1972.

De Aquiros, Felipe Torroba Bernaldo. *The Spanish Jews.* Madrid: S. A. Paseo Onesimo Redondo, 1972.

De Lange, N. R. M. *Origen and the Jews: Studies in Jewish-Christian Relationships.* London: Cambridge University Press, 1976.

Dimont, Max I. *Jews, God and History.* New York: Simon & Schuster, 1961.

Disputation and Dialogue: Readings in the Jewish-Christian Encounter. Washington, D.C.: Ktav/Anti-Defamation League of B'nai B'rith, 1975.

Durant, Will. *The Reformation.* Volume 6, *The Story of Civilization.* New York: MJF Books, 1957.

Eban, Abba. *Heritage: Civilization and the Jews.* New York: Summit, 1984.

Encyclopedia Judaica. Jerusalem: Keter Publishing House, 1973.

Evans, Craig. A. and Donald A. Hagner. *Antisemitism and Early Christianity.* Minneapolis: Fortress Press, 1993.

Hay, Malcolm. *The Roots of Christian Anti-Semitism.* New York: Freedom Library Press, 1981.

Hilberg, Raul. *The Destruction of the European Jews.* New York: Holmes & Meier, 1985.

Hitler, Adolf. *Mein Kampf.* Trans. by Ralph Mannheim. Boston: Houghton Mifflin, 1971.

Jocz, Jakob. *The Jewish People and Jesus Christ.* 3rd edition. Grand Rapids: Baker Book House, 1949.

Johnson, Paul. *A History of the Jews.* New York: Harper & Row, 1987.

Kac, Arthur. *The Messianic Hope.* Grand Rapids: Baker Book House, 1975.

Kac, Arthur. *The Messiahship of Jesus.* Grand Rapids: Baker Book House, 1986.

Kac, Arthur. *The Spiritual Dilemma of the Jewish People.* Grand Rapids: Baker Book House, 1983.

Klausner, Joseph. *The Messianic Idea in Israel.* New York: Macmillan, 1955.

Larsen, David L. *Jews, Gentiles and the Church.* Grand Rapids: Discovery House, 1995.

Latourette, Kenneth S. *A History of Christianity.* Vol. 1, revised. New York: Harper & Row, 1975.

Liebman, Charles S. and Steven M. Cohen. *Two Worlds of Judaism.* New Haven and London: Yale University Press, 1990.

Lieske, Bruce. *Witnessing to Jewish People.* St. Louis: Board of Evangelism Service of the Lutheran Church–Missouri Synod, 1984.

Michener, James A. *The Source.* New York: Fawcett Crest Books, 1967.

Potok, Chaim. *Wanderings.* New York: Fawcett Crest Books, 1978.

Riggins, Walter. *The Covenant with the Jews: What's So Unique About the Jewish People?* Tunbridge, Wells, England: Monarch Publications, 1992.

Rosenberg, Stuart E. *The New Jewish Identity in America.* New York: Hippocrene Books, 1985.

Roth, Cecil. *A History of the Marranos.* New York: Shocken Books, 1974.

Runes, Dagobert D., ed. *The Hebrew Impact on Western Culture.* New York: Philosophical Library of New York, 1951.

Sachar, Abram Leon. *A History of the Jews.* New York: Alfred A. Knopf, 1965.

Scholem, Gershon. *The Messianic Idea in Judaism.* New York: Shocken Books, 1971.

Standard Jewish Encyclopedia. New York: Doubleday, 1959.

Stoner, Peter, contrib. *Science Speaks.* Chicago: Moody Press, 1963.

Telushkin, Joseph. *Jewish Literacy.* New York: William Morrow, 1991.

Union Prayerbook for Jewish Worship. Part II. New York: The Central Conference of American Rabbis, 1962.

Universal Jewish Encyclopedia. New York: Universal Jewish Encyclopedia, 1939.

Wine, Sherwin T. *Judaism Beyond God.* Hoboken: KTAV Publishing House, 1995.

Wolf, Arnold Jacob. *Challenge to Confirmands.* New York: Scribe Publications, 1963.

World Almanac and Book of Facts, 1995. Funk & Wagnalls Corporation, 1994.

Yaseen, Leonard C. *The Jesus Connection.* New York: Crossroad, 1985.